Healthy Dutch Oven Cookbook:

150 Dutch Oven Recipes for Two Easy One Pot Meals

by

Noah White

Copyright © [Noah White]

All rights reserved. No part of this guide may be reproduced in any form without permission in writing from the publisher except in the case of brief quotations embodied in critical articles or reviews.

Table of Contents

Introduction 10
Chapter 1 Dutch Oven 11
Chapter 2 Breakfast and Brunch 14
Peanut Butter-Chia Oatmeal 14
Breakfast Potatoes 15
Shakshuka Eggs 16
French Toast Casserole 17
Chile Chilaquiles 18
Frittata 19
Donuts 20
Hash Brown Breakfast Casserole 21
Breakfast Burritos 22
Mexican Beef with Poached Eggs 23

Chapter 3 Snacks, Apps, and Sides 24
Herbed Goat Cheese Dip in Cocottes 24
Barbecue Baked Beans with Bacon 25
Corn Fritters with Chutney 26
Wild Rice Pilaf with Pistachios and Raisins 28
Sauteed Garlic Bok Choy 29
Roasted Brussels Sprouts with Harissa 30
Broiled Garlic-Herb Mashed Potatoes 31
Chipotle Black Beans 32
Artichoke Dip 33
Buffalo-Style Cauliflower 34

Chapter 4 Soups, Stews, and Chilis...............35

Tomato Bisque with Shrimp 35

Creamy Broccoli Soup... 36

Vegetable and Lentil Soup.. 37

Cauliflower-Leek Potage.. 38

Pork Green Chili... 39

Black Bean Soup with Citrus 40

Turmeric Vegetable Soup 41

Chicken and Rice Soup 42

French Onion Soup 43

Chipotle Turkey Chili 44

Bone Broth Beef Stew 45

Stewed Collard Greens with Beans and Ham 46

Chicken Pozole Verde 47

Three-Bean Chili 48

Chapter 5 Vegetables 49

Lasagna with Sauce... 49

Eggplant and Feta Shakshuka..51

Ratatouille 52

Pasta Puttanesca 54

Mac & Cheese with Breadcrumbs 55

Smoked Tofu and Corn Chili... 57

Dutch Oven Ravioli... 58

Cauliflower and Chickpea Tikka Masala 59

Vegan Rice Pilaf..60

Leek and Mushroom Risotto 61

Vegetarian Cassoulet 62

Vegetarian Stroganoff 63

Pasta with Pancetta and Sauce 65

Ratatouille II 67

Butternut Squash Chili 68

Chapter 6 Pasta, Rice and other Grains 70

Ginger-Scented Rice 70

Spanakorizo 71

Quinoa and Kale Salad 72

Salmon Congee with Sesame 73

Rigatoni with Pesto 74

Polenta with Mushrooms 75

Beef and Tomato Goulash 76

Beef Stroganoff 77

Soba Noodle Salad 78

Mac and Cheese 79

Chapter 7 Beef 81

Pot Roast with Vegetables 81

Flat Iron Steak 82

Korean Style Braised Short Ribs 83

Short Ribs in Red Wine 84

Beer-Braised Brisket 85

Steak with Vegetables and Blue Cheese 87

Greek Style Burger 88

Red Wine Steak 89
Steak Seared in Brown Butter 90
Flank Steak Fajitas 91
Grandma's Pot Roast 92
Beef and Veggie Soup... 93
Beef with Pineapple Curry 94
Dutch Oven Beef Steak Stew 95
Dutch Oven Beef Broccoli Stew... 96

Chapter 8 Chicken, Duck and Turkey 97

Chicken in Tomato Gravy 97
Creamy Chicken Breasts and Vegetables 98
Chicken Bean Chili... 99
Duck Carrot Noodle Soup.. 100
Chicken and White Bean Chili 101
Moroccan Chicken and Sweet Potatoes.. 102
Duck with Olive Sauce 104
Wild Duck Gumbo Stew 105
Duck and Sausage Cassoulet 106
Turkey, Bean & Corn Chili... 109
Mexican Turkey Soup 110
Turkey Meatballs in Cranberry Sauce 111
Turkey Shepherd's Pie 112
Braised Turkey Legs and Apples..113
Turkey Curry..114

Chapter 9 Pork and Lamb......................... 116

Noodles with Pork 116

Pork Piccata 117

Pork Medallions with Mustard Sauce 118

Chorizo-Stuffed Peppers 119

Pork Chili Verde with Rice 120

Pork Ribs Cacciatore 121

Stuffed Bacon-Wrapped Pork Tenderloin 123

Lamb Shanks with White Beans 124

Roasted Rack of Lamb and Baby Potatoes 125

Lamb Tomato Zucchini Stew 126

Greek Lamb Stew with Orzo 127

Lamb Shanks with Vegetables 128

Spanish Lamb Stew 129

Shepherd's Pie 130

Lamb Curry 131

Chapter 10 Fish and Seafood 133

Salt-Crusted Citrus Snapper 133

Spice-Rubbed Salmon 134

Steamed Mussels with Bacon 134

Spanish Paella 135

Lemon-Grilled Halibut with Salad 137

Grilled Swordfish Steaks 138

Linguine with Clams 139

Salmon with Spinach 140

Grouper with Vegetables 141

Bouillabaisse 142

Crispy White Fish with Sauce 143

Salmon Poached in Olive Oil 144

Halibut in Tomato Sauce with Chorizo 145

Roasted Cod with Potatoes and Olives 146

Crispy Salmon with Lemon-Butter Sauce 147

Chapter 11 Bread and Other Baked Goods ..148

Jalapeno Corn Bread with Honey Butter 148

Cherry and Dark Chocolate Scones 149

Honey-Jalapeno Cornbread 150

Fluffy Buttermilk Biscuits 151

Irish Soda Bread 152

Savory Cornbread 153

Parmesan Olive Bread 154

Seeded Dinner Rolls 155

Lemon Bread 156

Coconut Bread 157

Chapter 12 Desserts 159

Rhubarb & Strawberry Crisps 159

Chocolate Bread Pudding 160

Almond Cake 161

Mixed Berry Bake 162

Pear & Cranberry Crumble 163

Classic Bread Pudding 164

Deconstructed Apple Pie 165

Mango Sticky Rice 166

Cookies and Cream Ice Cream Cake 167

Buttermilk Cherry Clafoutis 168

Chapter 13 Staples and Sauces 169

Mild Red Enchilada Sauce 169

Smoky Paprika Cream Sauce 170

Caramel Sauce 171

Chile Nacho Cheese Sauce 171

Peanut Satay Sauce 172

Enchilada Sauce 173

Lemon Garlic Butter Sauce 174

Béchamel Sauce 174

Arrabbiata Sauce 175

Jalapeno Mango Chutney 176

Conclusion 177

Introduction

There are a lot of fancy kitchen tools available these days, and it is easy to overlook the Dutch oven. However, the Dutch oven is a versatile cooking appliance that can cook virtually anything and is really simple to use. The Dutch oven is the perfect cooking vessel. The simple but effective structure of this cooking appliance makes it ideal for everything from braising and stewing to simmering and casseroles. The Dutch oven is your go-to kitchen essential for one-pot meals. This book offers a variety of delicious recipes for delectable one-pot meals. This Dutch oven cookbook has something for everyone.

The Dutch oven is the predecessor of the slow cooker and can cook one-pot dishes, soups, stews, bread, baked goods, and even desserts. This cookbook includes familiar dishes, but the Dutch oven techniques and results will make you a Dutch oven fan. This Dutch oven cookbook has you covered for breakfast, lunch, snacks, appetizers, dinner, and even desserts! With this cookbook and your Dutch oven, you will discover how satisfying one-pot meals can be. Whether you are a new or seasoned cook, you will learn everything you need to know to make fresh, flavorful dishes at your home. The recipes use ingredients that you can find in your local grocery store.

The Dutch oven is the ultimate cooking appliance for simple meals, and this cookbook shows how extremely easy it is to cook mouthwatering meals. Ready your Dutch oven and use this cookbook for cooking amazing Dutch oven meals quickly and easily. Get started today with this Dutch oven cookbook and impress family and friends this winter and holiday season with heartwarming, mouthwatering meals.

Chapter 1 Dutch Oven

Dutch ovens have been around for over 300 years, and they are still used by many people for cooking. The Dutch oven began to conquer the United States in the 19th century. It has thick walls made of cast iron and a tightly fitting lid. It is very versatile and, when closed, is like a mobile oven. Everything that can be prepared in the oven can be prepared in this pot. In summary, a Dutch oven is an oven, pot, pan, and baking tray in one.

Dutch oven maintenance:

- o Many Dutch ovens are dishwasher-safe, but constant dishwashing may lead to some dulling of the enamel finish. Ideally, you should wash your Dutch oven by hand with soapy water.
- o Allow your cookware to cool before washing. This way, you will avoid thermal shock.
- o For light stains, rub with a dampened cloth and baking soda.
- o For more persistent stains, fill the pot with warm water and let it soak for 15 to 20 minutes before washing.
- o To remove stubborn, baked-on food residue, soak the pot overnight. Then clean.
- o Never store the Dutch oven while still dump
- o Periodically check handles and knobs to see if any of them are loose.
- o The porcelain finish of the Dutch oven can be damaged if the pot is banged or dropped on a hard surface or floor.

The type:

You have two basic options for a Dutch oven: "camp" or "stove." Your best choice will depend on what type of cooking you will be doing.

DIAMETER (IN INCHES)	QUARTS	WEIGHT (IN POUNDS)	MATERIAL	SERVES
8	2	8	Cast iron	1 or 2
9¾	4½	9.6	Enameled cast iron	2 to 4
11	6	13	Cast iron	2 to 5
13½	6	13	Enameled cast iron	4 to 6
11½	7¼	12.8	Enameled cast iron	6 to 10

Size:

If you are cooking for two, then a 4 or 5-quart pot is enough. If you want to cook pork shoulder or a whole chicken, then a 6 to a 7-quart pot is ideal.

Brand:

Le Creuset is considered the Rolls-Royce of Dutch ovens.

Here are a few reasons why you should use a Dutch oven

1. It has a large capacity and can accommodate a lot of food.
2. It goes from the stovetop to the oven. This makes cooking easier for you.
3. It saves time and cleanup.
4. It is budget-friendly.
5. Ensures even browning of food
6. You get flavorful meals
7. You can cook a single dish at multiple temperatures

8. This pot is extremely versatile

Chapter 2 Breakfast and Brunch

Peanut Butter-Chia Oatmeal

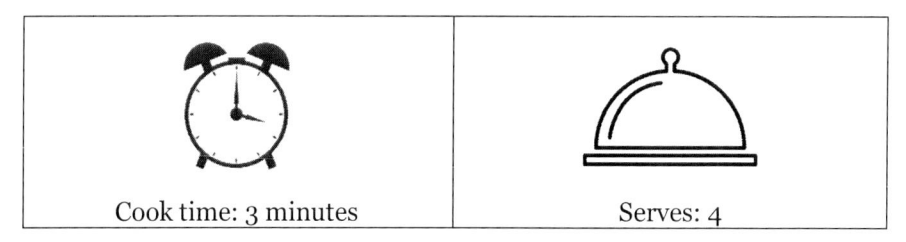

Cook time: 3 minutes	Serves: 4

Ingredients:

- 4 cups of water
- ¼ tsp. salt
- 2 cups quick-cooking oats
- ¼ cup creamy peanut butter
- 1 ripe banana, sliced
- 4 ounces fresh berries of choice
- Chia seeds, for garnish
- Honey or brown sugar, for serving

Directions:

1. In a Dutch oven, combine the water and salt and bring to a boil.
2. Cook the oats for 2 minutes. Stirring occasionally. Turn off the heat.
3. Add the peanut butter and garnish with the remaining ingredients.
4. Serve.

Breakfast Potatoes

Cook time: 40 minutes	Serves: 4

Ingredients:

- 3 large Yukon gold potatoes, cubed
- Pinch salt plus ½ tsp., divided
- 1 tbsp. olive oil
- 1 white onion, roughly chopped
- 1 orange bell pepper, roughly chopped
- 4 garlic cloves, smashed
- 1 tsp. ground turmeric
- ½ tsp. smoked paprika
- Freshly ground black pepper

Directions:

1. Preheat the oven to 425F.
2. Add water and salt to the Dutch oven and boil the potatoes for 3 minutes or until partially cooked. Then drain.
3. Clean the Dutch oven and add oil, onion, bell pepper, and garlic. Cook for 2 minutes. Add the potatoes and the remaining ingredients.
4. Mix and roast, uncovered, in the oven for 28 minutes.
5. Serve.

Shakshuka Eggs

Cook time: 15 minutes | Serves: 6

Ingredients:

- 1 tbsp. olive oil
- ½ yellow onion, finely chopped
- 1 red bell pepper, finely chopped
- 2 (14-ounce) cans fire-roasted diced tomatoes with garlic
- 2 tbsps. tomato paste
- 2 tsps. paprika
- 1 tsp. ground cumin
- 6 large eggs
- 1 tbsp. finely chopped fresh parsley
- Salt to taste
- Freshly ground black pepper
- Toast, for serving (optional)

Directions:

1. In a Dutch oven, combine the olive oil, onion, and red bell pepper. Cook for 3 minutes and stir in the tomatoes with their juices, tomato paste, paprika, and cumin. Cook for 2 minutes more.
2. Crack the eggs in this mix and cover the pot. Cook for 6 minutes.
3. Season with salt, pepper, and parsley.
4. Serve.

French Toast Casserole

Cook time: 50 minutes	Serves: 6

Ingredients:

- Unsalted butter, for preparing the Dutch oven
- 1 (1-pound) day-old loaf challah bread, sliced
- 4 large eggs
- 1¾ cups half-and-half
- ⅓ cup pure maple syrup, plus more for serving (optional)
- 1 tbsp. brandy
- 1 tsp. grated orange zest
- ½ tsp. salt
- 1½ cups frozen mixed berries

Directions:

1. Preheat the oven to 350F. Coat the inside of the Dutch oven with butter.
2. Arrange the bread slices in the Dutch oven, overlapping them.
3. Whisk the eggs, half-and-half, maple syrup, brandy, orange zest, and salt to combine.
4. Add the berries and pour the egg mixture over the bread.
5. Cover and bake for 40 minutes. Then remove the lid and cook for 10 minutes more.
6. Serve with maple syrup.

Chile Chilaquiles

Cook time: 10 minutes	Serves: 4

Ingredients:

- ¼ cup refined coconut oil
- 10 corn tortillas, cut into eighths
- ½ tsp. salt
- 1 (24-ounce) jar salsa verde
- ½ cup crumbled Cotija or Monterey cheese
- 1 tbsp. finely chopped fresh cilantro
- ¼ cup sour cream

Directions:

1. Melt the coconut oil in the Dutch oven.
2. Fry the tortillas in batches (about 1 minute per batch). Remove and sprinkle with salt.
3. Add the salsa to the Dutch oven and place the browned tortillas on top.
4. Cook for 2 minutes on medium heat.
5. Turn the heat off and sprinkle the cheese over the tortillas.
6. Garnish with sour cream and cilantro and serve.

Frittata

Cook time: 25 minutes	Serves: 6

Ingredients:

- 12 large eggs
- 3 tbsps. whole milk
- ½ tsp. salt
- 1 tbsp. olive oil
- 8 ounces (½ cup) jarred roasted bell peppers, roughly chopped
- 4 ounces goat cheese, crumbled

Directions:

1. Preheat the oven to 425F.
2. Whisk together the eggs, milk, and salt.
3. Add the oil to the Dutch oven and heat over medium heat.
4. Add the egg mixture and cook for 2 minutes. Stir continuously.
5. Spread the red bell peppers and goat cheese over the top of the frittata before the eggs set. Remove from the heat.
6. Transfer the Dutch oven to the oven and bake for 18 minutes, or until baked.
7. Cool, slice, and serve.

Donuts

Cook time: 20 minutes | Serves: 6

Ingredients:

- ½ cup lukewarm water
- 3 tbsps. sugar
- 1 tsp. active dry yeast
- 1 large egg
- ½ tsp. salt
- 3 tbsps. whole milk or half-and-half
- 2⅓ cups bread flour, plus more for dusting
- 1 tbsp. shortening
- 4 cups refined coconut oil, plus more for preparing the bowl
- ⅓ cup powdered sugar

Directions:

1. In a bowl, stir together the sugar, yeast, and water. Set aside for 5 minutes.
2. Add the egg, salt, and milk to the activated yeast and gently mix.
3. Add the flour, shortening, and stir to make a dough.
4. Knead the dough. Coat a bowl with oil and put the dough in it. Cover the bowl with a clean cloth and allow the dough to rise for at least 2 hours.
5. Warm the oil in the Dutch oven.
6. Roll the dough into a large ¼ inch thick rectangle and cut into rows. Then fry the rectangles into the hot oil in batches.
7. Dust with sugar and serve.

Hash Brown Breakfast Casserole

Cook time: 1 hour 5 minutes	Serves: 6

Ingredients:

- 1-pound ground sausage
- ½ yellow onion, finely chopped
- 1 bell pepper, any color, chopped
- 1 (20-ounce) bag frozen shredded hash browns, thawed
- Salt to taste
- Freshly ground black pepper
- 8 large eggs
- 1⅓ cups whole milk
- 2 cups shredded cheddar cheese
- Pickled jalapeño pepper slices, for garnish

Directions:

1. Preheat the oven to 350F.
2. Cook the sausage in the Dutch oven for 4 minutes or until browned.
3. Turn off the heat and add the onion, bell pepper, and hash browns. Season with salt and pepper.
4. Whisk the eggs and milk until smooth.
5. Pour the egg mixture over the hash brown casserole and top with the cheese and jalapenos.
6. Bake for 1 hour or until cooked.
7. Serve.

Breakfast Burritos

Cook time: 15 minutes | Serves: 6

Ingredients:

- 6 (12-inch) flour tortillas
- 2 tbsps. canola oil, divided
- 1-pound chorizo
- ½ yellow onion, finely chopped
- Salt to taste
- 1 cup shredded frozen hash browns
- Freshly ground black pepper
- 8 large eggs
- 1 cup shredded cheddar cheese
- Salsa, for serving

Directions:

1. Preheat the oven to 300F.
2. Spread the tortillas on a baking sheet and bake for 10 to 15 minutes.
3. Heat 1 tbsp. oil in the Dutch oven and add chorizo, onion, and salt.
4. Cook for 4 minutes and remove.
5. Add 1 tbsp. oil to the Dutch oven and cook the hash browns for 5 minutes. Do not stir.
6. Then flip the hash browns and season with salt and pepper. Cook for 3 minutes more. Transfer to a small bowl.
7. Cook the eggs in the Dutch oven for 3 minutes. Season and remove from the heat.
8. Assemble the burritos and serve.

Mexican Beef with Poached Eggs

Cook time: 25 minutes	Serves: 4

Ingredients:

- 1 lb. ground beef (80% lean)
- ½ red bell pepper, diced
- 4 eggs
- 1 small white onion, finely chopped
- ½ cup Mexican salsa
- 1 tsp cumin ½ tsp cayenne
- 2 tbsps. vegetable oil
- Salt and pepper to taste
- Coriander leaves (for garnishing)

Directions:

1. Preheat the Dutch oven.
2. Add oil and sauté the onion for 5 minutes.
3. Add ground beef and seasonings and sauté until brown.
4. Add the salsa and cook for 5 minutes. Season with salt and pepper.
5. Add the eggs on top and cover with the lid.
6. Cook for 10 minutes.
7. Open and garnish.
8. Serve.

Chapter 3 Snacks, Apps, and Sides

Herbed Goat Cheese Dip in Cocottes

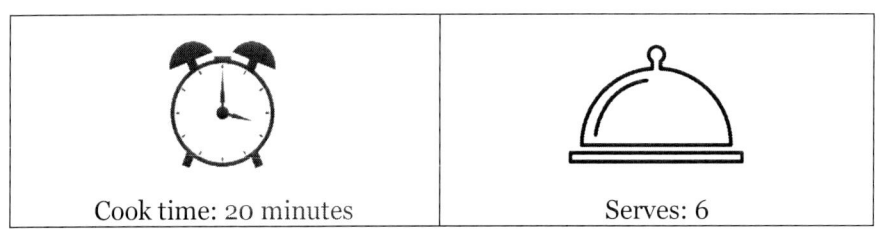

Cook time: 20 minutes	Serves: 6

Ingredients:

- Butter or oil for preparing the mini cocottes
- 5 ounces goat cheese
- 2 ounces cream cheese
- 2 ounces Greek yogurt
- ½ cup grated Gruyère cheese, divided
- 1 tbsp. olive oil
- 1½ 24 sps. balsamic vinegar
- 1 tbsp. minced flat-leaf parsley
- 1 tsp. minced fresh sage
- 1 tsp. minced fresh thyme
- 2 garlic cloves, minced
- Salt and ground black pepper to taste
- Baguette, pita chips, crackers, or vegetables, for dipping

Directions:

1. Preheat the oven to 375F. Coat two 12-ounce mini cocotte with butter or oil. Set aside.

2. In a bowl, combine the goat cheese, cream cheese, yogurt, ¼ cup Gruyere cheese, olive oil, vinegar, parsley, garlic, and thyme. Mix and season with salt and pepper.
3. Spoon the cheese mixture into the prepared cocotte. Then top with the remaining ¼ cup Gruyere cheese.
4. Bake for 20 minutes.
5. Serve with items for dipping.

Barbecue Baked Beans with Bacon

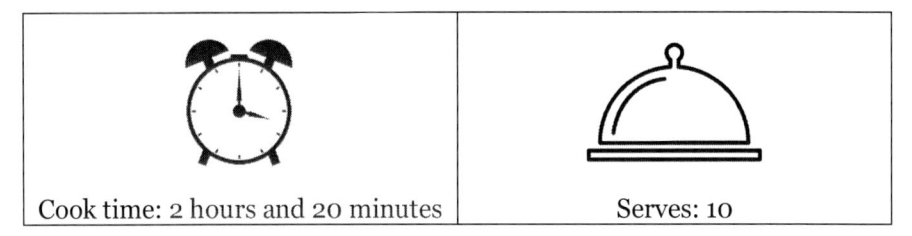

Cook time: 2 hours and 20 minutes	Serves: 10

Ingredients:

- 1 tbsp. vegetable oil
- 1 large onion, chopped
- 2 garlic cloves, minced
- 1½ cups ketchup
- ½ cup (packed) light brown sugar
- ½ cup light molasses
- ½ cup whole-grain mustard
- ¼ cup Worcestershire sauce
- 1 tbsp. hot pepper sauce
- 2 cups of water
- Salt and ground black pepper to taste
- 3 (15-ounce) cans navy or great northern beans, drained and rinsed
- 6 slices bacon, halved crosswise

Directions:

1. Preheat the oven to 350F.
2. Heat the oil in a Dutch oven.
3. Add onion and garlic and cook for 5 minutes.
4. Lower heat and stir in the brown sugar, ketchup, molasses, mustard, Worcestershire sauce, hot pepper sauce, and water. Season with salt and pepper.
5. Bring to a simmer and cook for 10 to 15 minutes.
6. Add the bacon and lay the bacon slices on top in a single layer.
7. Cover and bake for 2 hours. Serve.

Corn Fritters with Chutney

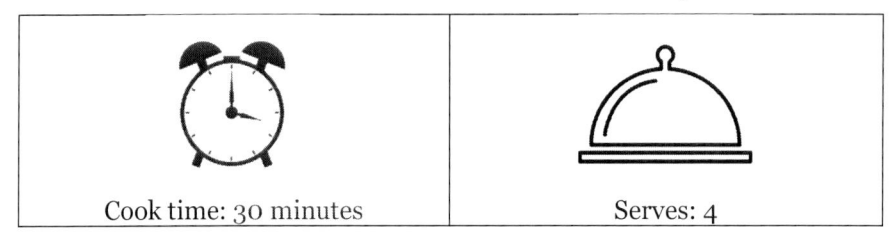

Cook time: 30 minutes	Serves: 4

Ingredients:

For the chutney

- 2 cups (packed) cilantro sprigs
- 1 cup (packed) fresh mint leaves
- ½ small onion, chopped
- ¼ cup of water
- 1 tbsp. freshly squeezed lime juice
- 1 fresh green chile
- 1 tsp. sugar

For the fritters

- 2 quarts peanut or vegetable oil, for frying
- ¾ cup all-purpose flour
- ½ cup medium-ground cornmeal
- 2 tsps. baking powder
- 1 tbsp. curry powder
- ¾ tsp. kosher salt
- ¼ tsp. cayenne pepper
- ¾ cup whole milk
- 1 large egg
- 4 ears corn, shucked and kernels cut from the cob
- 5 scallions, white and light green parts only, thinly sliced

Directions:

1. To make the chutney, blend the chutney ingredients in a blender until mostly smooth.
2. To make the fritters – in the Dutch oven, heat the oil until temperature reaches 360F. Line a plate with paper towels.
3. In a bowl, whisk together the cornmeal, flour, baking powder, curry powder, salt, and cayenne.
4. Whisk together the milk and egg in a bowl.
5. Add the egg mixture to the flour mixture and mix well. Add the corn kernels and scallions and stir to mix.
6. Drop the batter by the heaping tbsp. into the oil. Cook in batches.
7. Serve with chutney.

Wild Rice Pilaf with Pistachios and Raisins

Cook time: 50 minutes

Serves: 8

Ingredients:

- 2 tbsps. unsalted butter
- 1 tbsp. vegetable oil
- 3 large shallots, minced
- 2 cups wild rice
- 4 cups broth
- ½ cup raisins
- 1 bay leaf
- 2 sprigs fresh thyme sprigs
- ½ tsp. kosher salt
- ⅛ tsp. black pepper
- ½ cup coarsely chopped pistachios
- ¼ cup minced flat-leaf parsley

Directions:

1. Preheat the oven to 375F.
2. Heat the butter with oil in the Dutch oven.
3. Add the shallots and cook for 3 minutes.
4. Stir in the rice and coat with oil.
5. Add the raisins, broth, bay leaf, thyme, salt, and pepper, and bring to a simmer.
6. Cover and bake for 45 minutes or until rice is cooked.
7. Discard the bay leaf and thyme springs.
8. Garnish with pistachios and parsley and serve.

Sauteed Garlic Bok Choy

Cook time: 10 minutes	Serves: 4

Ingredients:

- 6 heads baby bok choy, trimmed and stem ends removed
- 2 tbsps. olive oil
- ½ tsp. salt
- 4 garlic cloves, minced
- Pinch red pepper flakes
- Juice of ½ lemon

Directions:

1. Heat the oil in a Dutch oven. Cook the bok choy with salt for 2 minutes without stirring.
2. Add the garlic and red pepper flakes and toss to coat.
3. Cook, undisturbed, for 2 minutes more.
4. Serve with lemon.

Roasted Brussels Sprouts with Harissa

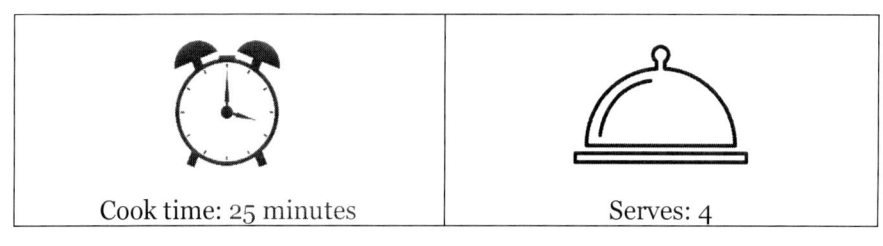

Cook time: 25 minutes	Serves: 4

Ingredients:

- 1 ½ pounds of Brussels sprouts, trimmed and halved
- 2 tbsps. olive oil
- ½ tsp. salt
- Harissa, for seasoning
- 1 lemon

Directions:

1. Preheat the oven to 425F.
2. In a Dutch oven, toss together the Brussels sprouts, olive oil, and salt.
3. Spread the sprouts in an even layer.
4. Roast the sprouts, uncovered, for 22 minutes.
5. Remove the pot from the oven and toss the sprouts with harissa to taste.
6. Grate the zest on top and drizzle with lemon juice.
7. Serve.

Broiled Garlic-Herb Mashed Potatoes

Cook time: 35 minutes	Serves: 6

Ingredients:

- 3 pounds russet potatoes, peeled and cubed
- 1 tbsp. salt, plus more for seasoning
- 6 tbsps. unsalted butter, divided
- 5 garlic cloves, minced
- 2 thyme sprigs
- 2 rosemary sprigs
- Freshly ground black pepper to taste

Directions:

1. Put the potatoes in a large pot with salt. Cover with water and bring to a boil over high heat. Cook for 20 minutes or until potatoes is fork-tender. Drain.
2. Melt 5 tbsps. butter in the Dutch oven. Add garlic, thyme, and rosemary.
3. Cook for 1 minute and turn off the heat.
4. Mash the potatoes and season with salt and pepper.
5. Melt 1 tbsp. butter in a bowl in the microwave.
6. Preheat the broiler.
7. Discard the thyme and rosemary springs from the Dutch oven.
8. Pour the potatoes into the Dutch oven and mix.
9. Add the remaining butter and place the Dutch oven directly under the broiler.
10. Broil until the top is golden brown.
11. Serve.

Chipotle Black Beans

Cook time: 10 minutes	Serves: 6

Ingredients:

- 2 dried chipotle chiles
- 2 tbsps. olive oil
- 1 white onion, finely chopped
- 2 garlic cloves, minced
- 2 tsps. ground cumin
- 1½ tsps. salt, plus more for seasoning
- 2 (15-ounce) cans black beans, drained and rinsed
- Lime juice, for seasoning

Directions:

1. Cook the chiles in the Dutch oven for 30 seconds.
2. Add the olive oil and onion and cook for 5 minutes.
3. Stir in the garlic, cumin, and salt.
4. Add the black beans and simmer for 5 minutes.
5. Taste and season with lime juice.
6. Remove and discard the chiles.
7. Serve.

Artichoke Dip

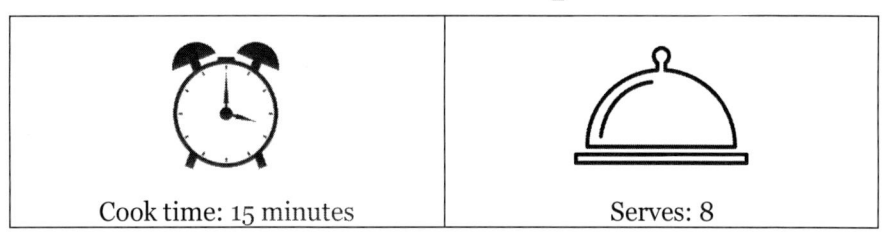

Cook time: 15 minutes

Serves: 8

Ingredients:

- 2 (14-ounce) cans artichoke hearts, drained and rinsed, chopped
- 2 cups mayonnaise
- 2 cups finely grated Parmesan cheese
- 1 tsp. freshly squeezed lemon juice
- ½ tsp. garlic powder

Directions:

1. Preheat the oven to 350F.
2. Place the artichoke hearts in the Dutch oven and stir in the mayonnaise, parmesan, lemon juice, and garlic powder to combine. Smooth the top.
3. Bake for 15 minutes.
4. Serve warm.

Buffalo-Style Cauliflower

Cook time: 25 minutes | Serves: 4

Ingredients:

- 2 tbsps. olive oil
- 1 head cauliflower, break into florets
- Salt and pepper, to taste
- 2 tbsps. unsalted butter
- ¼ cup Frank's red-hot sauce
- 1 tbsp fresh lime juice
- Chopped parsley or cilantro

Directions:

1. Preheat the oven to 375F.
2. Melt the butter in a bowl.
3. Add hot sauce and lime juice to the butter and stir.
4. Heat Dutch oven over low heat. Add oil and florets.
5. Sauté for 5 minutes.
6. Pour in hot sauce mixture and coat.
7. Place in the oven for 15 to 20 minutes or until cauliflower is softened.
8. Remove, garnish, and serve.

Chapter 4 Soups, Stews, and Chilis

Tomato Bisque with Shrimp

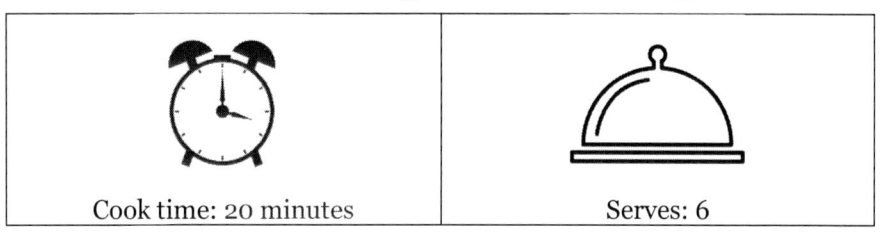

Cook time: 20 minutes	Serves: 6

Ingredients:

- 3 tbsps. olive oil
- 1 yellow onion, roughly chopped
- 2 celery stalks, roughly chopped
- 2 tsps. sea salt
- 1 tsp. freshly ground black pepper
- 1 garlic clove, minced
- 1 tsp. paprika
- 1 (28-ounce) can whole peeled tomatoes
- 1 (14-ounce) can full-fat coconut milk
- 8 ounces fresh shrimp, peeled and deveined

Directions:

1. Heat oil in the Dutch oven and add the onion, celery, salt, and pepper.
2. Sauté for 4 minutes or until tender.
3. Add the garlic and cook for 1 minute.
4. Add the paprika and cook for 1 minute more.
5. Add the milk and tomatoes with their juices. Cover and simmer for 5 minutes. Remove from the heat.
6. Blend the soup with a hand mixer.
7. Add shrimp to the hot soup and mix.
8. Cook for 2 to 3 minutes.
9. Serve.

Creamy Broccoli Soup

Cook time: 25 minutes	Serves: 6

Ingredients:

- ¼ cup olive oil
- ½ white onion, chopped
- 2 celery stalks, chopped
- 2 carrots, chopped
- 2½ tsps. salt
- 1 small russet potato, chopped
- 2 garlic cloves, minced
- 4 cups vegetable stock
- 1 large head broccoli, chopped
- ½ cup shredded cheddar cheese

Directions:

1. Heat a Dutch oven and add oil, onion, celery, carrots, and salt. Sauté for 3 minutes.
2. Add the garlic and potato and cook for 7 minutes. Stirring occasionally.
3. Add the stock and bring the soup to a simmer. Cook for 8 minutes.
4. Remove from the heat. Scoop out 2 cups of liquid from the pot and add it to the blender.
5. Add the broccoli florets to the blender, add cheese and blend on high until smooth and creamy.
6. Pour the blended soup back into the Dutch oven and bring to a simmer.
7. Mix and remove from the heat.
8. Garnish and serve.

Vegetable and Lentil Soup

Cook time: 25 minutes	Serves: 6

Ingredients:

- 3 tbsps. olive oil
- 1 onion, chopped
- 2 carrots, chopped
- 2 celery stalks, chopped
- 1 tbsp. garam masala, plus more for seasoning
- 1 tbsp. salt, plus more for seasoning
- 2 tsps. curry powder, plus more for seasoning
- 1 tsp. freshly ground black pepper, plus more for seasoning
- 6 cups of water
- 2 cups lentils

Directions:

1. Warm the oil in the Dutch oven.
2. Add the onion, carrots, and celery.
3. Sweat the vegetables for 7 minutes.
4. Stir in the garam masala, salt, curry powder, and pepper.
5. Cook for 2 minutes.
6. Pour the water over the vegetables and add the lentils. Stir, then cover. The pot and simmer for 15 minutes.
7. Add the seasoning and serve.

Cauliflower-Leek Potage

Cook time: 45 minutes	Serves: 6

Ingredients:

- 1 head cauliflower, cut into florets
- 1 tbsp. sea salt, plus more as needed
- Juice of 1 lemon, divided
- 2 leeks, sliced
- 2 tbsps. olive oil
- 4 cups vegetable stock
- Freshly ground black pepper
- 4 tbsps. unsalted butter
- ¼ cup slivered almonds
- Freshly grated nutmeg to taste

Directions:

1. Fill the Dutch oven about halfway with water and add the cauliflower, salt, and juice of ½ a lemon. Bring to a boil and cook for 15 minutes. Drain.
2. Heat the olive oil in the Dutch oven and add the leeks and salt. Cook for 15 minutes. Add the cooked cauliflower and vegetable stock and bring to a simmer.
3. Transfer the cauliflower and leeks to a blender and add a bit of liquid. Blend until very smooth. Return the puree to the Dutch oven.
4. Taste and adjust seasoning. Drizzle with lemon.
5. Combine the butter and almonds in a skillet and cook for 5 minutes.
6. Pour the browned butter into the soup and use almonds as garnish. Garnish with nutmeg and serve.

Pork Green Chili

Cook time: 1 hour 40 minutes | Serves: 6

Ingredients:

- 2 tbsps. olive oil
- 2 pounds boneless pork shoulder, chopped
- 2 tsps. salt
- 1 tsp. dried oregano
- 1 tsp. ground cumin
- 1 tsp. onion powder
- 1 tsp. ground coriander
- 1 cup salsa verde
- ½ cup sour cream
- 1 (4-ounce) can diced green chiles
- 1 cup of water
- 1 (15-ounce) can black beans, drained and rinsed

Directions:

1. Warm the olive oil in a Dutch oven. Add the pork and season with salt,
2. Cook for 3 minutes or until brown on all sides.
3. Stir in oregano, cumin, onion powder, and coriander. Cook for 30 seconds.
4. Pour in the salsa verde, sour cream, chilies, and water. Mix.
5. Cover and lower the heat. Simmer the soup for 1 ½ hour.
6. Add the black beans, adjust seasonings, and serve.

Black Bean Soup with Citrus

Cook time: 20 minutes | Serves: 4

Ingredients:

- 3 tbsps. olive oil
- 1 onion, chopped
- 1 red bell pepper, chopped
- 2 celery stalks, chopped
- 6 garlic cloves, chopped
- 2 tsps. ground cumin
- 1 tsp. chili powder
- 1 tsp. salt
- 2 (15-ounce) cans black beans, drained and rinsed
- 2 cups of water
- Grated zest and juice of 1 orange
- Juice of 2 limes
- Chopped fresh cilantro, for garnish

Directions:

1. Heat a Dutch oven and add oil, onion, bell pepper, and celery. Cook for 7 minutes.
2. Add the garlic, cumin, chili powder, and salt.
3. Coat and add black beans and water.
4. Bring the soup to a simmer and cook for 8 minutes.
5. Stir in orange juice, orange zest, and lime juice.
6. Garnish and serve.

Turmeric Vegetable Soup

Cook time: 20 minutes	Serves: 6

Ingredients:

- 2 tbsps. olive oil
- 1 sweet potato, peeled and diced
- 1 tsp. salt, plus more for seasoning
- 2 garlic cloves, minced
- 1 poblano chile, seeded and chopped
- 2 cups frozen corn
- 1 tbsp. chili powder
- 1 tsp. ground cumin
- 1 tsp. ground turmeric
- ½ cup dry white wine
- 4 cups of water
- 1 (14-ounce) can coconut milk

Directions:

1. Warm the olive oil in a Dutch oven.
2. Add the sweet potato and stir.
3. Combine and cook for 7 minutes. Stir in garlic, poblano, and corn. cook for 3 minutes.
4. Add the chili powder, cumin, and turmeric.
5. Mix and cook for 1 minute.
6. Stir in the white wine and deglaze the pot.
7. Add the water and bring the soup to a simmer. Cook for 5 minutes.
8. Season and serve.

Chicken and Rice Soup

Cook time: 30 minutes	Serves: 6

Ingredients:

- 1 leek, chopped
- 1 tbsp. olive oil
- 2 garlic cloves, minced
- 6 thyme sprigs
- 1 bay leaf
- 8 cups chicken stock
- ½ cup long-grain white rice
- Salt to taste
- 2 cups shredded rotisserie chicken
- 2 cups of frozen mixed vegetables
- Freshly ground black pepper
- Fresh parsley, for garnish

Directions:

1. Heat the oil in the Dutch oven and cook the leek for 4 minutes.
2. Add the garlic and cook for 2 minutes more.
3. Add the thyme, bay leaf, chicken stock, rice, and salt.
4. Stir and cover the pot. Cook for 15 minutes or until the rice is tender.
5. Add the chicken and vegetables and simmer for 3 minutes.
6. Season with salt and pepper and remove the bay leaf.
7. Garnish and serve.

French Onion Soup

Cook time: 45 minutes

Serves: 6

Ingredients:

- 8 tbsp. unsalted butter
- 4 white onions, thinly sliced
- 1 tsp. salt, plus more for seasoning
- 2 garlic cloves, minced
- 3 tbsps. all-purpose flour
- 1 cup dry red wine
- 2 bay leaves
- 1 tsp black pepper, plus more for seasoning
- 1 tsp. dried thyme
- 8 cups beef stock
- 4 cups grated Gruyère cheese
- Fresh parsley, for garnish

Directions:

1. Add the butter, onion, and salt to the Dutch oven.
2. Cook for 20 minutes, or until the onions are mostly brown.
3. Add the flour, wine, and garlic.
4. Cook for 1 minute.
5. Stir in the flour and cook for 3 minutes.
6. Add the red wine and cook for 1 minute, or until the wine has reduced by half.
7. Add the bay leaves, pepper, and thyme.
8. Increase heat and simmer for 10 minutes.
9. Taste and adjust seasoning.
10. Preheat the broiler and melt the cheese.

11. Position an oven rack under the broiler.
12. Top the cheese with cheese and broil for 3 minutes or until golden brown.
13. Garnish the soup with parsley and serve.

Chipotle Turkey Chili

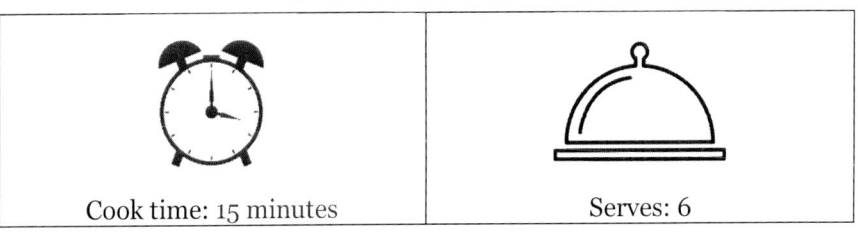

Cook time: 15 minutes	Serves: 6

Ingredients:

- 2 tbsps. olive oil
- 1 white onion, chopped
- 2 tbsps. chipotle powder
- 1 tbsp. ground cumin
- 1 tbsp. garlic powder
- 1 tsp. salt
- 1-pound ground turkey
- 1 (24-ounce) jar chunky mild salsa
- 2 (15-ounce) cans red kidney beans, drained and rinsed

Directions:

1. Warm the oil in a Dutch oven.
2. Add the onion and cook for 4 minutes.
3. Stir in the cumin, chipotle powder, garlic powder, and salt. Cook for 1 minute.
4. Add the ground turkey and cook for 3 minutes.
5. Pour the salsa over the turkey and mix.
6. Add the kidney beans and cover the pot.
7. Simmer for 5 minutes.
8. Serve.

Bone Broth Beef Stew

Cook time: 2 hours 45 minutes	Serves: 6

Ingredients:

- 3 pounds boneless beef chuck, cut into bite-size cubes and patted dry
- Salt and black pepper to taste
- 3 tbsps. olive oil
- 2 white or yellow onions, chopped
- ¼ cup of water
- 4 garlic cloves, minced
- 1½ tbsps. tomato paste
- 3 tbsps. all-purpose flour
- 2 cups dry red wine
- 2 cups beef bone broth
- 2 tsps. Italian seasoning
- 1-pound small white potatoes, peeled and chopped
- 4 carrots, chopped
- Fresh parsley, for garnish

Directions:

1. Season the beef with salt and pepper. Warm the oil in the Dutch oven.
2. Cook the beef in batches in the Dutch oven for 5 to 10 minutes per side. Remove to a bowl.
3. Add onions to the Dutch oven and cook for 6 minutes. Add water if needed.
4. Stir in the garlic and tomato paste and return the beef with its juice to the pot, along with the flour. Cook for 2 minutes.

5. Stir in the red wine, bone broth, and Italian seasoning. Cover the pot and reduce the heat. Simmer for 1 hour and 30 minutes.
6. Add the carrots, potatoes, salt, and pepper to taste.
7. Recover the pot and simmer the stew for 45 minutes.
8. Garnish and serve.

Stewed Collard Greens with Beans and Ham

Cook time: 1 hour	Serves: 6

Ingredients:

- 1 cup dried black-eyed peas
- 4 bacon slices, roughly chopped
- 1 yellow onion, chopped
- 3 carrots, chopped
- 5 garlic cloves, chopped
- 2 cups chicken stock
- 2 cups chopped cooked ham, smoked
- 3 cups of water
- 1 bunch collard greens, rinsed and chopped
- 1 tbsp. apple cider vinegar
- Salt and black pepper to taste

Directions:

1. Soak the black-eyed peas in water overnight. Drain.
2. Cook the bacon in the Dutch oven for 3 minutes.
3. Add the garlic, carrots, and onion. Cook for 5 minutes.
4. Add the ham, stock, drained peas, and water.
5. Cover and simmer for 50 minutes.
6. Add the vinegar and collard greens to the pot. Cook until wilted. Taste and adjust seasoning. Taste peas to make sure they are cooked. Serve.

Chicken Pozole Verde

Cook time: 15 minutes	Serves: 6

Ingredients:

- 1 tbsp. olive oil
- 1-pound boneless, skinless chicken thighs, chopped into bite-size pieces
- 1 tsp. salt, plus more for seasoning
- 3 tomatillos, husked, rinsed, and roughly chopped
- 2 serrano chiles, seeded and roughly chopped
- 1 white onion, roughly chopped
- 2 tsps. dried oregano
- 4 cups chicken stock
- 1 handful fresh cilantro
- 1 (29-ounce) can white hominy (no need to drain)

Directions:

1. Warm the oil in the Dutch oven.
2. Season the chicken with a pinch of salt and add to the pot.
3. Cook for 5 minutes or until browned on all sides. Transfer chicken to a bowl.
4. Combine the serranos, tomatillos, onion, oregano, salt, and chicken stock in the Dutch oven.
5. Increase heat and simmer for 5 minutes.
6. Add the cilantro and blend the soup with a hand mixer until smooth.
7. Return the chicken with its juices to the pot and add the hominy.
8. Simmer for 5 minutes and serve.

Three-Bean Chili

Cook time: 15 minutes | Serves: 4

Ingredients:

- 2 tbsps. olive oil
- 1 white onion, chopped
- 2 tbsps. chili powder
- 1 tbsp. ground cumin
- 1 tbsp. garlic powder
- 1 tsp. salt
- ½ tsp. ground coriander
- 1 (15-ounce) can red kidney beans, drained and rinsed
- 1 (15-ounce) can black beans, drained and rinsed
- 1 (15-ounce) can pinto beans, drained and rinsed
- 1 (24-ounce) jar chunky mild salsa
- Chopped fresh cilantro, for garnish
- Shredded cheese of choice, for serving

Directions:

1. Heat the oil in the Dutch oven until hot.
2. Add the onion and cook for 3 minutes.
3. Stir in the cumin, chili powder, garlic powder, salt, and coriander. Cook for 1 minute.
4. Pour in salsa and mix. Add the beans and cover.
5. Simmer for 7 minutes.
6. Top with cilantro and cheese and serve.

Chapter 5 Vegetables

Lasagna with Sauce

Cook time: 1 hour and 15 minutes	Serves: 4

Ingredients:

- 1 tbsp. olive oil
- 3 garlic cloves, minced
- 1 onion, diced
- Salt and pepper to taste
- 4 cups milk, divided
- ¼ cup cornstarch
- 2 (5-ounce) packages fresh baby spinach
- ½ cup chopped flat-leaf parsley, plus additional for garnish
- ¼ tsp. grated nutmeg
- 12 lasagna noodles, cooked according to package directions
- 1 medium butternut squash (about 2½ pounds), peeled, halved lengthwise, seeded, and sliced
- 2 cups shredded mozzarella cheese, divided
- ½ cup grated Parmesan cheese

Directions:

1. Preheat the oven to 400F.
2. Heat the oil in the Dutch oven.

3. Add the garlic and onion and season with salt and pepper.
4. Cook for 10 minutes.
5. Meanwhile, whisk together ½ cup of milk and the cornstarch.
6. Heat the remaining 3 ½ cups of milk until it bubbles in a saucepan.
7. Stir in the cornstarch mixture and bring to a boil. Cook for 5 minutes, or until thickens.
8. Add the sautéed garlic and onion to the milk mixture along with the nutmeg, spinach, and ½ cup of parsley. Cook for 1 to 2 minutes or until the spinach wilts. Taste and adjust seasoning.
9. Spread about ¾ cup of sauce mixture over the bottom of the Dutch oven. Arrange three noodles, to cover the bottom. Lay one-third of the squash slices over the noodles. Then sprinkle with ½ cup of mozzarella cheese and top with ¾ cup of sauce. Repeat to create two more layers. Finish with parmesan cheese.
10. Cover and bake for 40 minutes. Then remove the lid and bake for another 15 minutes.
11. Garnish and serve.

Eggplant and Feta Shakshuka

Cook time: 15 minutes	Serves: 4

Ingredients:

- 1 large eggplant, cut into cubes
- 1 tbsp. salt, plus additional for seasoning
- 3 garlic cloves, minced
- ⅓ cup chopped flat-leaf parsley, plus additional for garnish
- ⅓ cup chopped cilantro, plus additional for garnish
- 1 tbsp. paprika
- 1 tsp. ground cumin
- 1 hot red chile, minced
- 2 tbsps. olive oil
- ½ onion, diced
- 4 tomatoes, roughly chopped
- 1 (14.5-ounce) tomato purée
- Juice of ½ lemon
- Black pepper to taste
- 4 large eggs
- 2 ounces crumbled feta cheese

Directions:

1. Place the eggplant in a strainer set over a bowl and toss it with 1 tbsp. salt. Let sit for about 10 minutes.
2. In a bowl, stir together the cumin, garlic, 1/3 cup of parsley, 1/3 cup of cilantro, paprika, and chile.

3. Rinse the eggplant and remove the excess moisture.
4. Heat the oil in the Dutch oven. Add the onion and cook for 5 minutes.
5. Add the eggplant and cook for 5 minutes more.
6. Stir in the tomato puree, tomatoes, lemon juice, and the garlic and spice mixture. Season with salt and pepper and bring to a simmer.
7. Cook, uncovered, for 15 minutes or until sauce thickens.
8. Form four divots on the surface of the vegetable mixture with a wooden spoon. Crack an egg into each divot and sprinkle with feta cheese over the top. Cover and cook for 6 minutes.
9. Garnish and serve.

Ratatouille

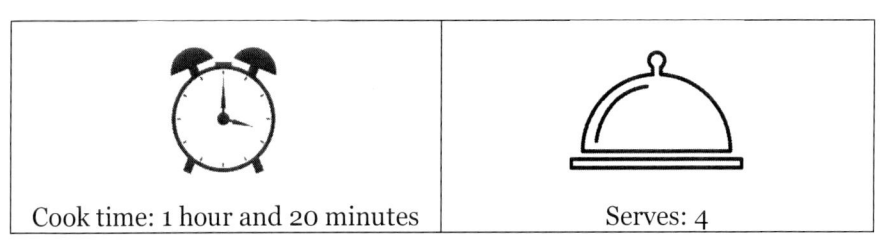

Cook time: 1 hour and 20 minutes	Serves: 4

Ingredients:

- 2 large eggplants, peeled and cut into cubes
- 1 tbsp. salt, plus additional for seasoning
- 5 tsps. olive oil, divided
- 2 onions, diced
- 2 red or green bell peppers, seeded and cut into strips
- 6 medium zucchinis, cut into cubes
- 4 garlic cloves, minced
- 4 large tomatoes, diced
- 1 bay leaf

- 4 sprigs fresh thyme
- 1 tbsp. red wine vinegar

Directions:

1. Place the eggplant cubes in a strainer set over a bowl. Toss with 1 tbsp. salt. Let sit for 15 minutes.
2. Heat 1 tsp. oil in a Dutch oven. Add the onions, season with salt, and cook for about 8 minutes or until browned.
3. Stir in the peppers and cook for 5 minutes. Transfer the peppers and onions to a bowl and set aside.
4. Add 1 tsp. oil to the pot along with zucchini and season with salt. Cook for 5 minutes. Add the zucchini to the bowl with peppers and onion.
5. Rinse the eggplant and squeeze to remove excess moisture.
6. Add 2 tsps. of the oil to the pot and cook the eggplant for 10 minutes or until softened. Add the eggplant to the bowl of the cooked vegetables.
7. Preheat the oven to 400F.
8. Heat the remaining 1 tsp. olive oil in a Dutch oven.
9. Add the garlic and cook for 1 minute.
10. Stir in the bay leaf, tomatoes, and thyme and bring to a simmer. Cook for 3 minutes.
11. Return all the vegetables to the pot and mix.
12. Transfer the pot to the oven and bake, uncovered, for 15 to 20 minutes or until bubbling.
13. Stir in the vinegar and adjust seasoning.
14. Remove and discard thyme springs and bay leaf.
15. Serve.

Pasta Puttanesca

Cook time: 15 minutes | Serves: 4

Ingredients:

- ¼ cup olive oil
- 3 garlic cloves, minced
- 4 anchovy fillets
- 1½ tsps. dried oregano
- ¾ tsp. red pepper flakes
- 24 Kalamata olives, pitted and chopped
- 3 tbsps. capers
- 4 cups vegetable broth
- 12 ounces dried penne
- 3 pints cherry or grape tomatoes, halved
- 2 tbsps. tomato paste
- ¼ cup chopped fresh basil
- ¼ cup chopped flat-leaf parsley
- ⅛ tsp. kosher salt
- Ground black pepper to taste
- Parmesan cheese, for serving

Directions:

1. Heat the oil in a Dutch oven.
2. Add garlic, anchovies, oregano, and red pepper flakes. Cook for 2 minutes.
3. Stir in capers and olives. Add the broth, dried pasta, and bring to a boil.

4. Cook, uncovered, for 10 minutes. Stirring occasionally.
5. Stir in tomatoes and tomato paste and continue to cook for 3 minutes or until the pasta is tender.
6. Remove the pot from the heat and stir in the salt, parsley, and basil.
7. Season with black pepper and serve with Parmesan cheese.

Mac & Cheese with Breadcrumbs

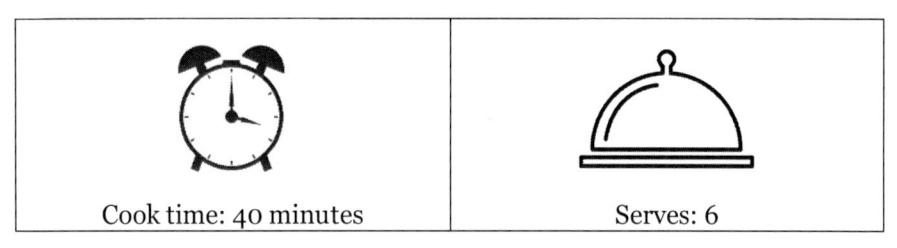

Cook time: 40 minutes	Serves: 6

Ingredients:

For the topping

- 2 tbsps. unsalted butter
- 2 tbsps. olive oil
- 2 cups panko breadcrumbs
- 2 garlic cloves, minced
- 2 ounces grated Parmesan cheese
- ½ tsp. kosher salt

For the mac and cheese

- ¼ cup unsalted butter
- 3 tbsps. all-purpose flour
- 2 cups whole milk
- 6 tbsps. heavy cream
- 2 tsps. mustard powder

- 1 tsp. salt
- ½ tsp. paprika
- ¼ tsp. cayenne pepper
- 14 ounces extra-sharp Cheddar cheese
- 2 ounces grated Parmesan cheese
- 4 cups dried elbow macaroni noodles, cooked al dente

Directions:

1. To make the topping: heat the butter with oil in the Dutch oven. Cook until the butter foams and then the foam subsides.
2. Stir in the garlic and breadcrumbs and cook for 5 minutes. Transfer the mixture to a bowl and stir in the parmesan cheese and salt.
3. To make the mac & cheese: preheat the oven to 400F.
4. Melt the butter in the Dutch oven. While whisking, drizzle the flour over the butter. Cook for 5 minutes. Whisk constantly.
5. Continue to whisk and add the milk and cream. Continue to whisk, increase heat, and bring the mixture just to a boil. Lower heat and simmer until the sauce thickens about 3 minutes. Whisk occasionally.
6. Stir in the salt, mustard powder, paprika, and cayenne.
7. 1 cup at a time, add the cheddar and parmesan cheese. Whisk after each addition. Melt completely and remove the pot from the heat.
8. Add the cooked and drained pasta to the cheese sauce and mix well.
9. Spread the mixture into an even layer and sprinkle the bread crumb topping on top.
10. Bake, uncovered for 20 minutes, or until the sauce is bubbling.
11. Rest for 10 minutes and serve.

Smoked Tofu and Corn Chili

Cook time: 40 minutes	Serves: 4

Ingredients:

- 2 tbsps. olive oil
- 1 large onion, diced
- 4 garlic cloves, minced
- 2 large poblano chiles, seeded and finely diced
- 1 large red bell pepper, seeded and chopped
- 1 jalapeño chile, seeded and minced
- ¼ tsp. chili powder
- 1 tsp. ground cumin
- 1 (28-ounce) can crushed tomatoes
- 1 cup canned tomato sauce
- ½ tsp. dried oregano
- 1 tsp. kosher salt
- 1-pound smoked tofu, diced
- 1 (19-ounce) can pinto beans, drained and rinsed
- 1½ cups fresh or frozen corn kernels
- ½ cup cilantro, for garnish

Directions:

1. Heat the oil in the Dutch oven.
2. Add the garlic, onions, chilies, bell pepper, and jalapenos and cook for 8 minutes.
3. Stir in chili powder and cumin and cook for 2 minutes more.

4. Add the tomato sauce, tomatoes, oregano, and salt and bring to a simmer. Reduce the heat to a gentle simmer and cook for 15 minutes.
5. Add the tofu and beans and cook for 10 minutes more.
6. Stir in the corn and simmer for 3 minutes more.
7. Garnish and serve.

Dutch Oven Ravioli

Cook time: 45 minutes	Serves: 6

Ingredients:

- 1 (25 oz.) bag of frozen cheese ravioli, thawed
- 1 large (45 oz.) spaghetti sauce
- 1 cup mozzarella cheese, grated
- ½ cup parmesan cheese, grated
- ½ cup of water

Directions:

1. Spray the Dutch oven with cooking spray or line with aluminum foil.
2. Pour a thin layer of spaghetti sauce on the bottom of the Dutch oven. Put a single layer of ravioli on the bottom of your Dutch oven.
3. Cover the ravioli with the remaining pasta sauce.
4. Sprinkle with a bit of parmesan cheese and place the second layer of ravioli on top. Top with the remaining parmesan and mozzarella cheese.
5. Pour the water around the sides of the Dutch oven to provide enough moisture.
6. Bake at 350F for 45 minutes. Serve.

Cauliflower and Chickpea Tikka Masala

Cook time: 25 minutes	Serves: 4

Ingredients:

- 2 tbsps. olive oil
- 1 onion, diced
- 4 garlic cloves, minced
- Pinch of salt
- 1 tbsp. garam masala
- 1 (2-inch) piece of fresh ginger, grated
- 1 fresh jalapeño chile, stemmed, seeded, and minced
- 1 (15-ounce) can chickpeas, drained and rinsed
- 2 (14.5-ounce) cans diced tomatoes
- 1 small head cauliflower, cut into florets
- 1 cup of full-fat coconut milk
- ¼ cup chopped cilantro, plus additional for garnish

Directions:

1. Heat the oil in the Dutch oven.
2. Add the garlic, onion, and salt and cook for 5 minutes.
3. Stir in the ginger, garam masala, and jalapeno and cook for 1 minute more.
4. Add the cauliflower, tomatoes, and chickpeas. Bring to a boil and then lower the heat to medium-low. Simmer for 15 minutes.
5. Stir in the coconut milk and simmer for 5 minutes more.
6. Remove the pot from the heat and stir in the cilantro.
7. Serve.

Vegan Rice Pilaf

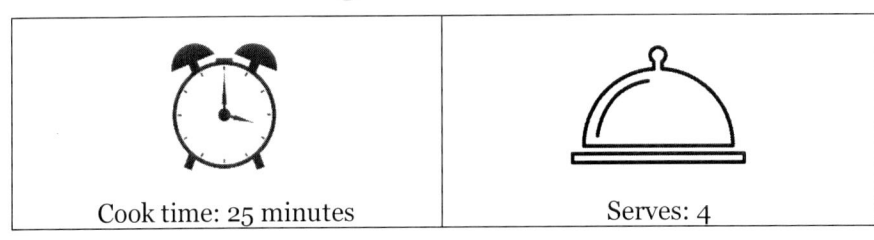

Cook time: 25 minutes	Serves: 4

Ingredients:

- 1 cup long-grain rice (basmati)
- ½ cup frozen peas
- 1 small white onion, chopped
- 1 ½ tsps curry powder
- 2 tbsps olive oil
- 2 cloves of garlic, minced
- ½ bunch cilantro leaves, roughly chopped
- 2 1/3 cups vegetable broth
- Salt and pepper to taste

Directions:

1. Heat oil in the Dutch oven. Add garlic, onion, and peas and cook for 5 minutes.
2. Add the rice and cook for 2 minutes. Add the broth and cover.
3. Cook for 20 to 25 minutes or until the rice has cooked fully and absorbed all the broth.
4. Fluff the rice, garnish and serve.

Leek and Mushroom Risotto

Cook time: 35 minutes | Serves: 4

Ingredients:

- 7 cups chicken broth
- 7 tbsps. of unsalted butter, divided
- 1½ pounds fresh wild mushrooms, sliced
- Salt and pepper to taste
- 1 tbsp. olive oil
- ¾ cup finely chopped leek (white and pale green parts only)
- 1¼ cups Arborio rice
- ½ cup dry white wine
- ¼ cup grated Parmesan cheese, plus additional for serving

Directions:

1. Bring the broth to a simmer in a saucepan and keep warm.
2. Melt 4 tbsps. of butter in the Dutch oven. Add the mushrooms and season with salt and pepper. Cook for 5 minutes. Transfer to a bowl.
3. Heat the remaining 3 tbsps. of butter with olive oil in the Dutch oven.
4. Add leek, season with salt, and cook for 5 minutes.
5. Increase heat to medium and add rice. Cook the rice for 3 minutes.

6. Add the wine and cook for 1 minute or until the liquid is fully absorbed.
7. ¾ cup at a time, begin adding the warm broth, stirring after each addition.
8. After about 10 minutes of adding broth ¾ cup at a time, stir in the mushrooms. Then add the remaining broth, ¾ cup at a time. Cook for 10 minutes, or the broth is mostly absorbed, and the rice is creamy and tender, but still al dente.
9. Garnish with parmesan and serve.

Vegetarian Cassoulet

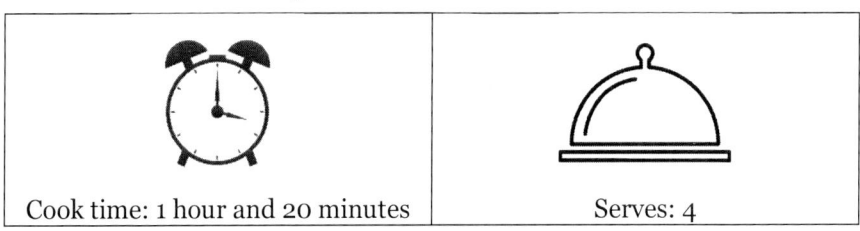

Cook time: 1 hour and 20 minutes	Serves: 4

Ingredients:

- 5 tbsps. olive oil, divided
- 3 garlic cloves, unpeeled
- 2 medium onions, sliced
- 1 tsp. salt, plus additional for seasoning
- 2 pounds cubed butternut squash
- 2 tbsps. red wine vinegar
- 2 (15-ounce) cans cannellini beans, drained and rinsed
- 1 cup vegetable broth
- 1 tbsp. chopped fresh thyme
- ½ tsp. ground black pepper
- 2 bay leaves

- 2 cups panko breadcrumbs
- ½ cup grated Parmesan cheese
- ¼ cup chopped flat-leaf parsley, for garnish

Directions:

1. Preheat the oven to 375F.
2. Heat 2 tbsps. oil in the Dutch oven.
3. Add the onions, garlic, and season with salt. Cook for 15 minutes and transfer to a bowl.
4. Heat 2 tbsps. of the remaining oil and add the beans, squash, broth, thyme, 1 tsp. salt, pepper, and bay leaves.
5. Stir together the breadcrumbs, parmesan cheese, and remaining 1 tbsp. of oil in a bowl. Sprinkle the breadcrumb mixture evenly over the bean mixture.
6. Cover and bake for 45 to 50 minutes.
7. Remove the lid and continue to bake, uncovered for 15 minutes more or until the topping is crisp and golden brown.
8. Garnish and serve.

Vegetarian Stroganoff

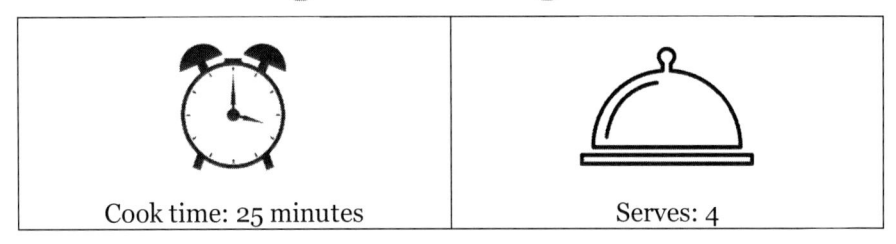

Cook time: 25 minutes	Serves: 4

Ingredients:

- ½ ounce dried porcini mushrooms
- 2 cups boiling water
- 8 ounces dried egg noodles
- 3 tbsps. olive oil, divided

- 8 ounces fresh cremini mushrooms, stems trimmed and sliced ¼-inch thick
- 1 onion, diced
- ½ tsp. paprika
- 2 tbsps. of all-purpose flour
- ¾ pound kale, tough center ribs removed and leaves julienned
- 3 garlic cloves, minced
- Salt and pepper to taste
- ¼ cup dry white wine
- 2 tbsps. unsalted butter
- ⅓ cup sour cream
- ¼ cup chopped flat-leaf parsley, for garnish

Directions:

1. Place the dried porcini in a bowl and pour the boiling water over them.
2. Soak the mushrooms for 10 minutes. Remove the mushrooms and reserve the soaking water. Chop the mushrooms. Strain 1 ½ cups of the mushroom soaking liquid. Reserve the gritty sediment that has settled on the bottom of the bowl. Discard the remaining sediment and soaking liquid.
3. In a pot, bring heavily salted water to a boil over high heat.
4. Cook the noodles according to the package directions. Reserve 1/3 cup of the cooking water and drain the noodles.
5. Heat 1 tbsp. oil in the Dutch oven. Add the cremini mushrooms and cook for 5 minutes. Transfer the mushrooms to a bowl and add the chopped porcini.
6. Reduce the heat to medium and add the remaining 2 tbsps. of oil.
7. Add the paprika and onion and cook for 5 minutes.

8. Sprinkle the flour over the onions and cook and stir for 2 minutes.
9. Stir in the garlic, kale, and season with salt and pepper. Cook for 1 minute.
10. Stir in the reserved mushrooms and their juices.
11. Add the wine and bring to a boil. Cook for 3 minutes or until most of the liquid has evaporated.
12. Lower the heat and add the reserved mushroom soaking liquid. Season with salt and pepper. Cook for 5 minutes or until sauce thickens.
13. Add the reserved pasta cooking water to the sauce and simmer for 2 minutes.
14. Stir in the butter and cook for 2 minutes more.
15. Remove the pot from the heat and add the sour cream. Stir to mix.
16. Garnish and serve.

Pasta with Pancetta and Sauce

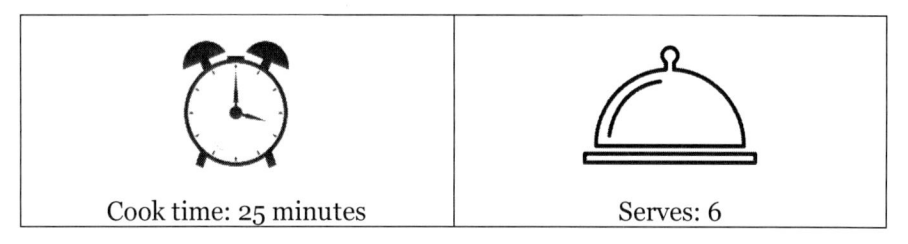

Cook time: 25 minutes	Serves: 6

Ingredients:

- 1 lb. penne pasta
- 1 ½ cups of cremini, quartered
- 4 oz. pancetta, chopped
- 1 large shallot, finely chopped
- 2 tbsps all-purpose flour
- 2 cloves of garlic, minced
- ½ cup heavy cream
- ½ cup dry white wine
- ⅔ cup goat cheese

- 1 ½ cup reserved pasta water
- Salt and pepper to taste

Directions:

1. Heat a Dutch oven and cook the pancetta for 5 to 7 minutes or until brown.
2. Remove the pancetta to a plate and keep the drippings in the Dutch oven.
3. Meanwhile, cook the penne pasta according to package instructions.
4. Add the shallots and garlic and cook for 2 minutes. Remove and toss aside.
5. Add the mushrooms with the oil and sauté for 7 to 8 minutes. Season with salt and pepper to taste.
6. Pour the wine into the Dutch oven with the mushrooms and deglaze. Cook until the wine has reduced by half. Add the goat cheese and stir well.
7. Add in the reserved pasta water and bring to a boil.
8. Then stir in the heavy cream and cook for 3 to 4 minutes. Stir in the kept shallots, garlic, and herbs.
9. Mix the pasta and pancetta with goat cheese sauce coat well.
10. Serve.

Ratatouille II

Cook time: 1 hour and 30 minutes	Serves: 4

Ingredients:

- 2 large Yukon potatoes, peeled and cut into cubes
- 2 large eggplants, peeled and cut into cubes
- 2 medium zucchinis, cubed
- 1 large white onion, chopped
- 2 tbsps lemon juice
- 2 cloves of garlic, minced
- 1 tbsp tomato paste
- 1 cup vegetable broth
- ½ tsp thyme
- ½ tsp oregano
- Salt and pepper to taste
- ¼ cup olive oil

Directions:

1. Pour the lemon juice over the eggplant cubes to take some of their bitterness out and season with salt and pepper.
2. Add the olive oil to the Dutch oven and heat. Add all the veggies and sauté for 3 to 4 minutes. Add the herbs and spices.
3. Add the vegetable broth and tomato paste to the Dutch oven with the veggies and cover the lid.
4. Bake in a 360F oven for 1 hour and 15 minutes.
5. Open the lid and continue to cook for another 15 minutes.
6. Serve.

Butternut Squash Chili

Cook time: 1 hour	Serves: 4

Ingredients:

- 3 red bell peppers, chopped
- 1 small butternut squash, peeled and cut into small cubes
- 1 medium red onion, sliced
- 4 cloves of garlic, minced
- 2 (15 oz.) cans black beans
- 1 tsp ground cumin
- ¼ tsp ground cinnamon
- 1 bay leaf
- 1 small can, diced tomatoes with juice
- 2 cups vegetable broth
- ½ chipotle pepper, sliced
- 2 ripe avocados, peeled and sliced
- 2 tbsps. olive oil
- Salt and pepper to taste

Directions:

1. Warm the oil in the Dutch oven.
2. Add the bell peppers, onion, and butternut squash and cook for 4 to 5 minutes or until onions are translucent.
3. Lower the heat and add garlic, chili powder, 1 tbsp. chipotle pepper and rest of the spices. Add the tomatoes, black beans, and bay leaf. Stir and add the vegetable broth. Cover and cook for 1 hour.

4. Garnish with avocado slices and serve.

Chapter 6 Pasta, Rice and other Grains

Ginger-Scented Rice

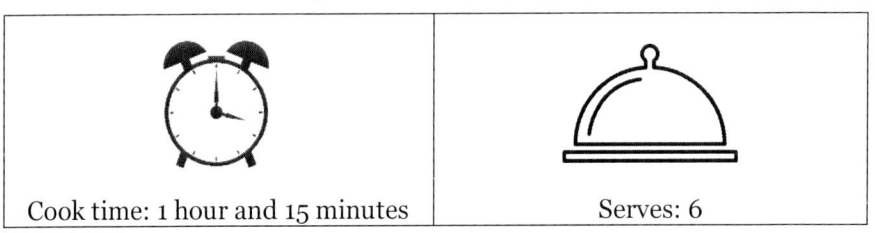

Cook time: 1 hour and 15 minutes	Serves: 6

Ingredients:

- 1 cup brown basmati rice
- 2 tsps. unrefined coconut oil
- 2 ¼ cups boiling water
- ½ tsp. salt
- 1-inch ginger, halved

Directions:

1. Preheat the oven to 375F.
2. Wash the rice and drain.
3. Cook the rice in the Dutch oven for 3 minutes, or until the grains are dry.
4. Add the coconut oil and stir to coat the rice.
5. Add the boiling water, salt, and ginger. Cover and bake in the oven for 1 hour or until the water is absorbed.
6. Remove the pot and let the rice steam, covered, for 10 minutes.
7. Fluff the rice and remove the ginger.
8. Serve.

Spanakorizo

Cook time: 1 hour	Serves: 6

Ingredients:

- ½ cup olive oil
- 1 yellow or white onion, chopped
- 6 scallions, thinly sliced
- 1 cup medium-grain brown rice
- ¼ cup freshly squeezed lemon juice
- 1 tbsp. finely chopped fresh dill
- 1 tsp. salt
- 2½ cups water
- 1-pound fresh baby spinach

Directions:

1. Heat the olive oil in the Dutch oven. Add the scallions and onion and sweat for 8 minutes or until soft.
2. Stir in the lemon juice, rice, dill, salt, and water. Bring to a boil over high heat.
3. Cover and lower heat to medium-low. Simmer for 40 minutes or until most of the water is absorbed.
4. Turn off the heat and stir in the spinach.
5. Cover the pot again and steam for 10 minutes.
6. Serve.

Quinoa and Kale Salad

Cook time: 35 minutes | Serves: 4

Ingredients:

- ¼ cup olive oil, plus more for seasoning
- 2 tbsps. pine nuts
- 2 garlic cloves, minced
- ¼ tsp. red pepper flakes
- 1 cup white quinoa
- 1 tsp. salt, divided
- 1¾ cups boiling water
- Juice of 3 lemons, plus more for seasoning
- 1 (2.25-ounce) can sliced black olives, drained
- 1 bunch curly kale, ribbed and roughly chopped
- 1 bunch fresh parsley, finely chopped
- 4 Roma tomatoes, seeded and chopped

Directions:

1. Combine the olive oil, pine nuts, garlic, and red pepper flakes in the Dutch oven. Warm for 2 minutes or until the nuts begin to lightly brown. Transfer to a bowl and set aside.
2. Rinse the quinoa and drain. Add the quinoa to the Dutch oven. Add ½ tsp. salt and boiling water. Bring to a boil over high heat.

3. Lower heat and cover. Simmer for 15 minutes. Remove from the heat and allow the quinoa steam, covered, for 10 minutes.
4. Add the lemon juice and the remaining ½ tsp. salt to the bowl with pine nuts and olive oil. Mix and add the kale, black olives, parsley, and tomatoes. Mix well.
5. Fluff the quinoa with a fork and a bit at a time, mix it into the kale salad.
6. Toss and adjust seasoning. Serve.

Salmon Congee with Sesame

Cook time: 45 minutes	Serves: 6

Ingredients:

- ¼ cup sesame seeds
- 4½ cups water
- ½ cup white basmati rice
- 1½ tsps. salt
- 8 ounces fresh salmon fillet, skin removed, cut into 1-inch pieces
- 1 tbsp. unsalted butter
- 1 tbsp. toasted sesame oil
- ½ cup thinly sliced fresh chives

Directions:

1. Cook the sesame seeds in the Dutch oven for 4 minutes or until they have a nutty smell. Stirring occasionally. Remove the seeds from the pot and set aside.

2. Combine the rice, water, and salt in the Dutch oven over high heat.
3. Bring to a boil and lower heat to maintain a simmer. Cook for 30 minutes, or until rice is tender. Stirring frequently.
4. Stir in the butter, salmon, and sesame oil. Cover the pot and cook for 5 minutes or until the salmon is pink and opaque.
5. Stir in the chives.
6. Garnish with sesame seeds and serve.

Rigatoni with Pesto

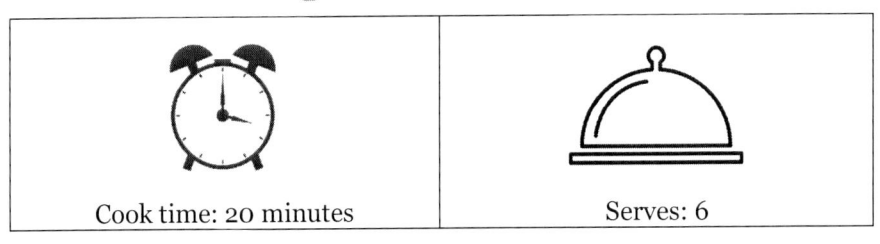

Cook time: 20 minutes | Serves: 6

Ingredients:

- Salt to taste
- 1-pound rigatoni pasta
- 1 cup raw pumpkin seeds
- 5 ounces fresh baby spinach and kale mix
- 3 garlic cloves, roughly chopped
- 1-ounce Pecorino Romano cheese, roughly chopped
- ½ cup olive oil
- ½ cup red wine vinegar
- 1 tsp. red pepper flakes
- Black pepper to taste

Directions:

1. Cook the pasta according to package directions until al dente. Drain.

2. Meanwhile, make the pesto. Add everything to a blender (except for the pasta) and blend until the mixture is mostly creamy with a bit of texture.
3. Toss the pasta with the pesto.
4. Taste and adjust seasoning.
5. Serve.

Polenta with Mushrooms

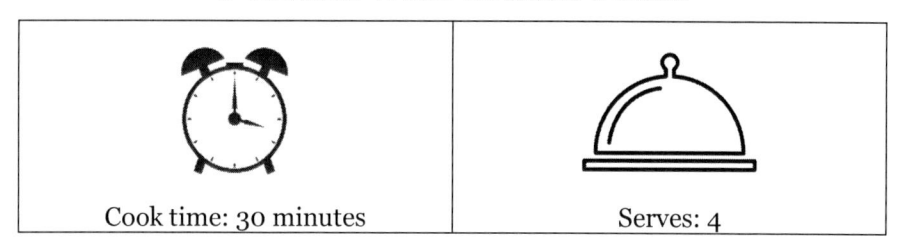

Cook time: 30 minutes	Serves: 4

Ingredients:

- 2½ cups vegetable stock
- 1 tsp. balsamic vinegar
- ½ tsp. salt, plus more for seasoning
- ¾ cup polenta corn grits
- ½ cup finely grated Parmesan cheese
- 8 ounces cremini mushrooms, thinly sliced
- 8 ounces shiitake mushrooms, thinly sliced
- 1 tsp. dried thyme
- 2 tbsps. olive oil
- Pinch red pepper flakes, for seasoning

Directions:

1. Preheat the oven to 450F.
2. In a Dutch oven, combine the vinegar, vegetable stock, and salt. Bring to a boil. Add the polenta and mix well.
3. Lower the heat to maintain a simmer and cook for 10 minutes or until creamy and tender.

4. Remove from the heat and stir in the parmesan. Smooth the top and set aside to firm.
5. In a bowl, mix the mushrooms, thyme, olive oil, and salt.
6. Spread the mushroom mixture over the polenta and roast for 15 minutes.
7. Serve.

Beef and Tomato Goulash

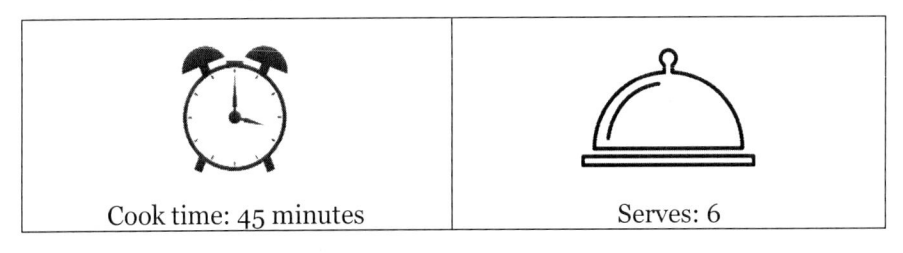

Cook time: 45 minutes	Serves: 6

Ingredients:

- 2 pounds lean ground beef
- 2 garlic cloves, minced
- 2 tbsps. Italian seasoning
- 1 tsp. salt
- ½ tsp. freshly ground black pepper
- 1 (14.5-ounce) can diced tomatoes
- 1 (26-ounce) jar pasta sauce
- 3 cups of water
- 3 tbsps. tamari
- 2 cups dried elbow macaroni
- 1 cup shredded cheddar cheese

Directions:

1. Cook the ground beef in the Dutch oven for 5 minutes. Stir in the garlic, Italian seasoning, salt, and pepper. Cook for 2 minutes.

2. Add the pasta sauce, tomatoes and their juices, water, and tamari. Cover the pot and simmer for 10 minutes.
3. Stir in the macaroni. Cover the pot and simmer for 20 minutes or until the pasta is just cooked.
4. Stir in the cheddar cheese and serve.

Beef Stroganoff

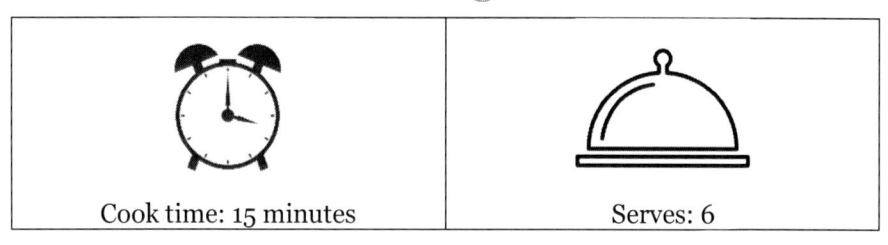

Cook time: 15 minutes	Serves: 6

Ingredients:

- Salt to taste
- 4 tbsps. unsalted butter, divided
- 2 pounds lean ground beef
- Black pepper to taste
- 1-pound egg noodles
- 1 yellow onion, finely chopped
- 4 garlic cloves, minced
- 1-pound cremini mushrooms, sliced
- ½ cup dry white wine
- 1 tbsp. Worcestershire sauce
- ½ cup sour cream
- Chopped fresh parsley, for garnish

Directions:

1. Bring a large pot of salted water to a boil.
2. Melt 2 tbsps. butter in the Dutch oven.

3. Add ground beef and season with salt and pepper. Cook for 4 minutes or until brown. Transfer the beef with its juices to a bowl and set aside.
4. Add the egg noodles to the boiling water and cook until al dente, about 8 to 10 minutes. Drain, but do not rinse.
5. Meanwhile, melt the remaining 2 tbsps. butter in the Dutch oven.
6. Add the onion and cook for 3 minutes. Stir in the mushrooms and garlic. Cook for 5 minutes.
7. Pour the wine and deglaze the pot.
8. Return the beef with its juices. Stir in the Worcestershire sauce and sour cream.
9. Garnish and serve.

Soba Noodle Salad

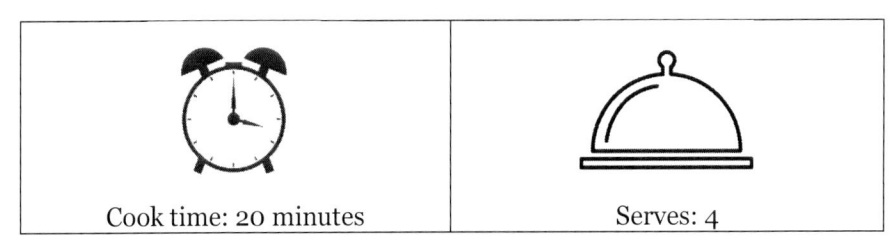

Cook time: 20 minutes	Serves: 4

Ingredients:

- Salt to taste
- 8 ounces gluten-free soba noodles
- ¼ cup sesame oil
- 8 ounces shiitake mushrooms, thinly sliced
- 2 heads bok choy, cut into ½-inch-thick slices
- 2 tsps. peeled and minced fresh ginger
- 1 tsp. red pepper flakes
- ¼ cup tamari
- ¼ cup rice vinegar

- 2 tbsps. brown rice syrup
- 2 tbsps. mirin

Directions:

1. Cook the soba noodles in the Dutch oven according to package instructions. Drain and rinse under cold water. Set aside.
2. Combine the shitake mushrooms and sesame oil in the Dutch oven. Cook for 3 minutes.
3. Stir in the ginger, bok choy, and red pepper flakes.
4. Sauté for 1 minute. Then add the vinegar, tamari, brown rice syrup, and mirin. Mix.
5. Serve.

Mac and Cheese

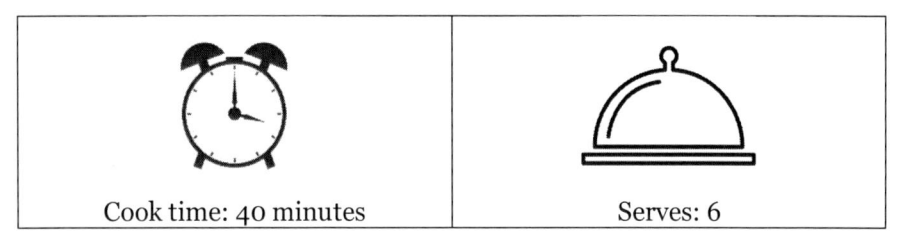

Cook time: 40 minutes	Serves: 6

Ingredients:

- 5 ounces Gouda cheese
- 5 ounces sharp cheddar cheese
- Salt to taste
- 1-pound large dried elbow macaroni
- 1 tbsp. olive oil
- 5 tbsps. unsalted butter
- ⅓ cup all-purpose flour
- 2½ cups whole milk
- 2 tsps. paprika

Directions:

1. Preheat the oven to 375F. Mix both the cheeses in a bowl. Set aside.
2. Cook the pasta in the Dutch oven 1-minute shy of al dente, according to the package instructions. Drain the pasta and add olive oil and toss to coat.
3. Melt the butter in the Dutch oven. Add flour. Whisk and cook for 2 minutes.
4. Slowly stir in the milk and bring the mixture to a simmer. Turn off the heat.
5. Add the pasta and cheese to the milk mixture. Coat well.
6. Sprinkle with paprika and bake for 15 minutes, or until golden and bubbly.
7. Serve.

Chapter 7 Beef

Pot Roast with Vegetables

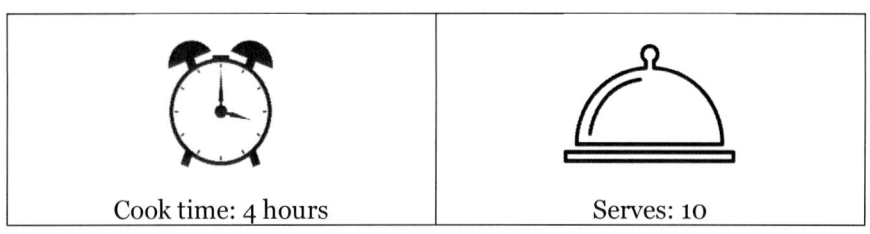

Cook time: 4 hours	Serves: 10

Ingredients:

- 1 (4-pound) chuck roast
- Salt and pepper to taste
- 2 tbsps. olive oil
- 2 onions, cut into wedges
- 6 carrots, peeled and cut into 2-inch lengths
- 1 cup dry red wine
- 3 cups beef broth
- 3 sprigs thyme
- 3 sprigs rosemary

Directions:

1. Preheat the oven to 275F.
2. Season the roast with salt and pepper.
3. Heat the oil in the Dutch oven. Add the onions and cook for 5 minutes. Transfer to a plate.
4. Add the carrots and cook for 3 minutes. Transfer the carrots to the plate with the onions.
5. Add the roast to the pot and cook for 5 minutes or until browned on all sides. Transfer to the plate with the vegetables. Add the wine to the pot and deglaze it.
6. Return everything in the pot and add broth, thyme, and rosemary.
7. Cover and roast for 3 ½ hours or until the roast is very tender. Rest for 10 minutes. Slice and serve.

Flat Iron Steak

Cook time: 16 minutes

Serves: 4

Ingredients:

- 1 tsp coarse salt
- 1 tsp paprika
- 1 tsp cumin
- 1 tsp garlic powder
- 1 tsp onion powder
- ½ tsp coriander
- ½ tsp thyme
- ¼ tsp black pepper
- 4 (6-oz) flat iron steaks
- 2 tbsps. olive oil

Directions:

1. Combine the first eight ingredients in a bowl and mix well.
2. Rub the seasoning mix onto the steaks and drizzle with 2 tbsps. olive oil.
3. Heat Dutch oven over medium heat.
4. Place steaks into the Dutch oven and sear for 3 minutes on each side. Cook for an additional 3 minutes for medium-rare. Rest and serve.

Korean Style Braised Short Ribs

| Cook time: 1 hour and 40 minutes | Serves: 6 |

Ingredients:

- 3 pounds bone-in beef short ribs, cut into ½-inch slices
- 1 onion, quartered
- 4 garlic cloves, peeled
- 1 tart apple, peeled, cored, and cut into quarters
- 1 (1-inch) piece fresh ginger, peeled
- ⅓ cup mirin
- ⅓ cup of soy sauce
- ⅓ cup brown sugar
- 1 tbsp. sesame oil
- 1 tsp. freshly ground black pepper
- ¼ to ½ tsp. cayenne pepper
- 1½ cups water
- 2 carrots, peeled and cut into 2-inch lengths
- 1 small radish, cut into 2-inch chunks

Directions:

1. Place the short ribs in the Dutch oven and cover with water. Bring to a boil over a high heat and cook for 5 minutes. Drain.
2. Combine the garlic, onion, apple, and ginger in a blender and process until smooth. Add the mirin and process to combine.
3. Return the ribs to the Dutch oven and pour the onion mixture over the top. Cook over low heat for 20 minutes.

4. Combine the soy sauce, brown sugar, sesame oil, black pepper, and cayenne in a bowl. Add this mixture and water to the meat and bring to a boil.
5. Lower heat and simmer covered for 45 minutes.
6. Stir in the radish and carrots, and continue to cook, covered for another 30 minutes or until the meat is very tender.

Short Ribs in Red Wine

Cook time: 3 hours and 30 minutes	Serves: 8

Ingredients:

- 5 pounds bone-in beef short ribs, cut crosswise into 2-inch pieces
- Salt and ground black pepper to taste
- 3 tbsps. vegetable oil
- 3 onions, diced
- 3 carrots, peeled and diced
- 2 celery stalks, diced
- 3 tbsps. all-purpose flour
- 1 tbsp. tomato paste
- 1 (750-milliliter) bottle dry red wine
- 10 sprigs flat-leaf parsley
- 8 sprigs thyme
- 4 sprigs oregano
- 2 bay leaves
- 4 cups beef broth
- ¼ cup minced flat-leaf parsley, for garnish

Directions:

1. Preheat the oven to 350F.
2. Season the meat with salt and pepper. Heat oil in a Dutch oven.
3. Cook the meat in the pot for about 8 minutes, or until browned on all sides. Then transfer to a plate. Drain off most of the rendered fat from the pot. Leave about 3 tbsps.
4. Add carrots, onions, and celery to the Dutch oven and cook for 5 minutes. Stirring frequently.
5. Add the tomato paste and flour and cook for 3 minutes or until the flour is mixed. Stirring continuously.
6. Add the ribs with their juices and add the red wine. Bring to a boil and lower heat. Simmer for 30 minutes or until the liquid is reduced by half.
7. Tie the thyme, parsley, oregano, and bay leaves together with a piece of kitchen twine. Tuck the bundle into the pot.
8. Add the broth and bring to a boil. Cover.
9. Transfer to the oven and bake for 2 ½ hours or until the meat is very tender.
10. Discard the herb bundle and transfer the ribs to a plate. Strain the sauce.
11. Garnish and serve.

Beer-Braised Brisket

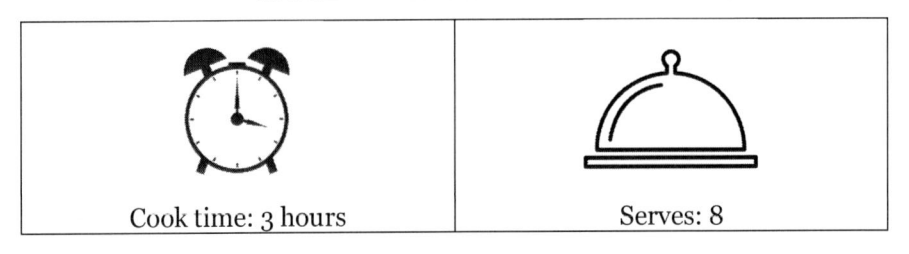

Cook time: 3 hours	Serves: 8

Ingredients:

- 2 tbsps. oil

- 1 (3-pound) beef brisket, trimmed of excess fat and silver skin
- Salt and pepper to taste
- 1 (2-inch) cinnamon stick
- 4 whole cloves
- 4 green cardamom pods, crushed
- 2 pounds white onions, sliced ½ inch thick
- 1½ tbsps. finely minced garlic
- 1½ tbsps. grated fresh ginger
- 1 (22-ounce) lager beer (such as Sapporo)
- 1 tbsp. dark brown sugar
- 1 cup beef broth
- 1 tsp. apple cider vinegar

Directions:

1. Preheat the oven to 325F.
2. Heat the oil in the Dutch oven.
3. Season the brisket with salt and pepper.
4. Add the brisket to the pot and cook for 10 minutes or until browned on all sides. Transfer the brisket to a plate.
5. Add the cloves, cinnamon stick, and cardamom pods into the pot and cook for 1 minute, or until fragrant.
6. Add the garlic, onions, and ginger, and salt. Cook for 10 minutes or until onions turns golden.
7. Add the beer and deglaze the pot. Stir in the sugar and return the brisket to the pot with its juices.
8. Add the broth and bring to a boil. Cover.
9. Transfer to the oven and cook for 2 ½ hours or until the meat is tender.
10. Remove the lid and continue to cook in the oven until the meat is very tender, about 20 to 30 minutes.
11. Remove the brisket from the pot and place it on a carving board. Tent with foil and rest for at least 10 minutes.
12. Stir the vinegar into the pot and mix. Taste and adjust seasoning.
13. Serve the brisket with sauce.

Steak with Vegetables and Blue Cheese

Cook time: 1 hour	Serves: 6

Ingredients:

- 2 tbsps. vegetable oil, divided
- 2 sweet onions, diced
- 2 garlic cloves, minced
- 2 cups mushrooms, thinly sliced
- 1½ tsps. kosher salt, divided
- 1½ tsps. black pepper, divided
- 2 pounds flank steak, butterflied
- 5 ounces baby spinach
- 6 ounces blue cheese, crumbled
- 2 tbsps. unsalted butter, divided
- 1 shallot, diced
- ¾ cup low-salt beef broth
- ½ cup dry red wine

Directions:

1. Preheat the oven to 350F.
2. Heat 1 tbsp. oil in a Dutch oven.
3. Add the garlic, onions, mushrooms, ½ tsp. salt, and ½ tsp. pepper. Cook for 20 minutes and remove the mixture to a bowl.
4. Lay the steak out flat. Then spread the vegetable mixture on top evenly. Crumble the blue cheese and top with spinach. Roll the steak and tie with kitchen twine. Season the steak with remaining salt and pepper.

5. Heat the remaining 1 tbsp. oil in the Dutch oven.
6. Add the steak and cook for 5 minutes, or until browned on all sides.
7. Transfer to the oven and bake for 12 minutes.
8. Remove the steak from the pot and transfer it to a cutting board.
9. Tent it with foil and rest for 10 minutes.
10. Meanwhile, make the sauce: melt 1 tbsp. butter in the Dutch oven.
11. Add the shallot and cook for 3 minutes.
12. Add the wine and broth and bring to a boil. Cook until the sauce is reduced to about ½ cup, about 10 minutes. Swirl in the remaining 1 tbsp. of butter.
13. Serve the steak with sauce.

Greek Style Burger

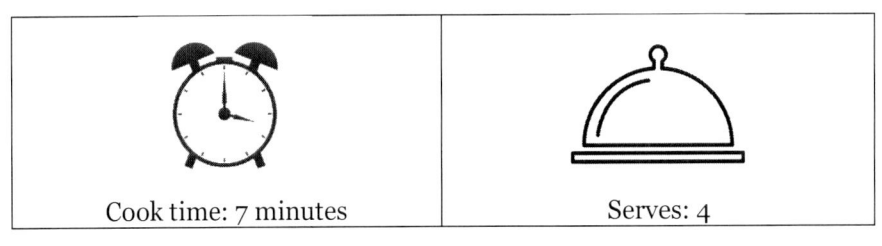

Cook time: 7 minutes	Serves: 4

Ingredients:

- 1½ lbs. ground sirloin or chuck
- 2 tsps. Worcestershire sauce
- ½ tsp dried oregano
- ½ cup crumbled feta cheese
- 1/3 cup finely diced red onion
- 1 tsp kosher salt
- ½ tsp black pepper
- Arugula to taste
- 4 tomatoes, sliced
- Tzatziki sauce to taste

- Oil as needed
- Buns for serving

Directions:

1. Preheat the Dutch oven.
2. Combine oregano, beef, Worcestershire sauce, feta cheese, onion, salt, and pepper in a bowl. Make 4 patties.
3. Place a small amount of vegetable oil in the Dutch oven.
4. Add burgers into the Dutch oven and cook 2 to 3 minutes per side.
5. Place burgers in buns and top with sauce, arugula, and sliced tomatoes.

Red Wine Steak

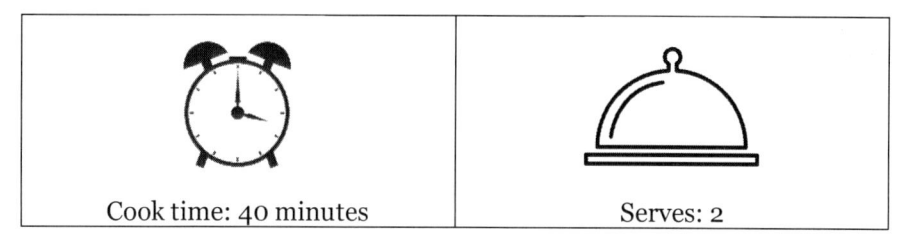

Cook time: 40 minutes	Serves: 2

Ingredients:

- 2 (8-oz) sirloin steaks, trimmed of fat
- Salt and pepper, to taste
- 4 tbsps. extra-virgin olive oil, divided
- 1 lb. fingerling potatoes, rinsed, halved
- 3 tbsps. shallots, minced
- 2 tsps. chopped fresh thyme
- ¾ cup red wine

Directions:

1. Pat the steaks dry with a paper towel. Season with salt and pepper.

2. Heat 1 tbsp. oil in the Dutch oven.
3. Add the potatoes and season with salt and pepper. Cook, covered on low heat for 20 to 30 minutes. Set aside.
4. Heat the remaining 3 tbsps. oil in the Dutch oven over a high heat. Then lower the heat to medium-high.
5. Add the steaks and cook for 4 minutes per side for medium-rare. Remove from the pot and set aside.
6. Add the thyme and shallots to the pot.
7. Add the wine and cook until the liquid is almost evaporated, about 1 to 2 minutes. Season with salt and pepper and stir.
8. Spoon the sauce over the steaks and serve with the potatoes.

Steak Seared in Brown Butter

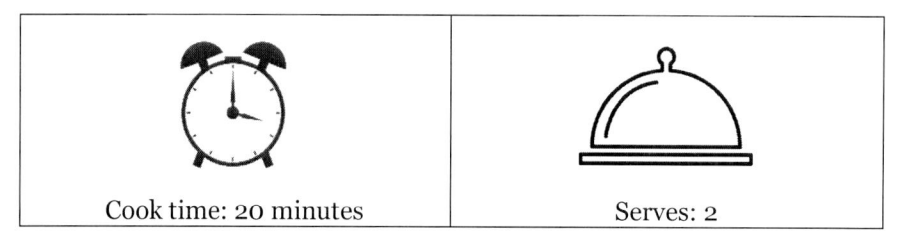

Cook time: 20 minutes	Serves: 2

Ingredients:

- 2 (1-lb) steaks, 1 inch thick (room temperature)
- 1 tbsp extra-virgin olive oil
- 3 tbsps. unsalted butter, divided
- 1 lb. Yukon gold potatoes, sliced about ½-inch thick
- 2 fresh rosemary sprigs
- Salt and black pepper, to taste
- ½ cup beef broth

Directions:

1. Heat the oil and 1 tbsp. butter in the Dutch oven.

2. Add the rosemary and potatoes and cook for 5 minutes. Season with salt and pepper. Remove from the pot and set aside.
3. Season the steak with salt and pepper.
4. Add the steak to the Dutch oven over high heat and cook for 5 minutes on each side for medium-rare.
5. Remove the steak and rest on a cutting board.
6. Melt the remaining 2 tbsps. butter over medium heat. Add the broth when the butter starts to brown. Keep stirring and deglaze the pot.
7. Add the potatoes and cook for 5 minutes.
8. Cut the steaks in half and spoon the potatoes and browned butter over each steak. Serve.

Flank Steak Fajitas

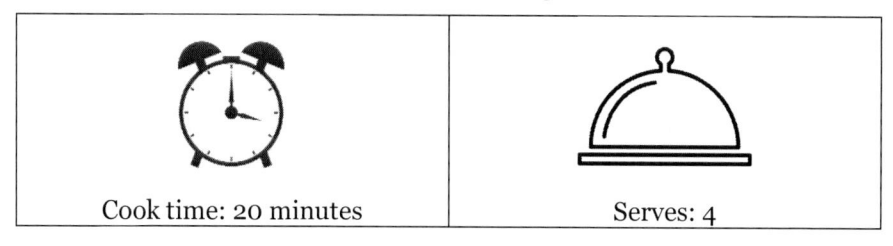

Cook time: 20 minutes	Serves: 4

Ingredients:

- 1 lb. flank or skirt steak
- 3 cloves garlic
- ½ cup of soy sauce
- ½ cup honey
- 3 sprigs rosemary
- Salt and pepper, to taste
- 2 limes, juiced
- 3 bell peppers, seeded and sliced
- 2 medium onions, peeled and sliced into rings
- 10 Portobello mushrooms, washed and sliced
- 4 flour tortillas

Directions:

1. Combine soy sauce, garlic, honey, rosemary, salt, pepper, and lime juice in a Ziploc bag. Add steak and marinate for 2 hours in the refrigerator.
2. Remove meat from the marinade and shake off excess liquid.
3. Heat the grill and sear the steak on the grill, 3 to 4 minutes per side.
4. Meanwhile, add 1 tbsp. oil to the Dutch oven and add peppers, onions, mushrooms, salt, and pepper. Cook and stir for 6 minutes.
5. Transfer both the steak and vegetables to a platter.
6. Place tortillas in the Dutch oven and toast for 30 seconds.
7. Serve.

Grandma's Pot Roast

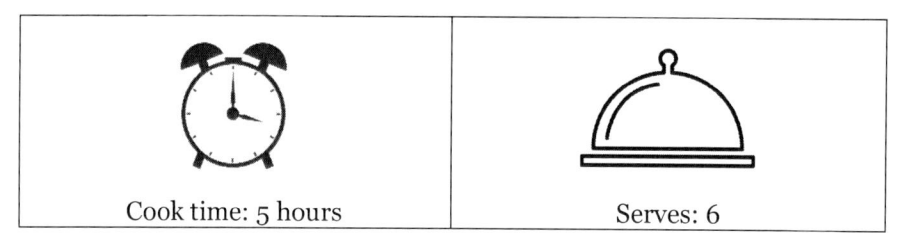

Cook time: 5 hours	Serves: 6

Ingredients:

- 5lb. beef chuck (for roasting)
- 6 large russet potatoes, washed, with the skin on
- 3 large carrots, sliced
- 2 red onions, cut into quarters
- ½ cup red wine
- 2 bay leaves
- 1 tbsp thyme
- 2 cups beef stock
- 2 cloves of garlic, peeled and halved
- 2 tbsps. olive oil

Directions:

1. Preheat the oven to 325F. Season the beef chuck with salt and pepper.
2. Add the olive oil to the Dutch oven and cook for 2 minutes per side (about 8 minutes).
3. Arrange the vegetables around the roast and place the garlic on top. Combine the red wine and broth. Pour over the top of the roast.
4. Sprinkle the thyme on top and add the bay leaves.
5. Cover and place in the oven. Roast for 4 ½ hours or until meat falls apart.
6. Serve.

Beef and Veggie Soup

Cook time: 50 minutes	Serves: 8

Ingredients:

- ⅔ lb. lean beef chucks, cubed
- 2 large carrots, sliced
- 1 large onion, sliced
- 1 large Yukon potato, cubed
- ⅔ cup white rice
- 3 tbsps. lemon juice
- 6 cups beef broth
- 2 tbsps. olive oil
- Salt and pepper to taste

Directions:

1. Heat the oil in the Dutch oven.
2. Sear the beef cubes until brown and add the onions. Sauté for 2 minutes.

3. Add all the rest of the ingredients and cover.
4. Cook for 45 minutes.
5. Serve.

Beef with Pineapple Curry

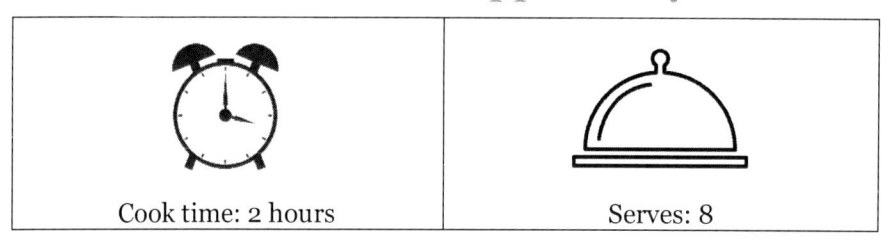

Cook time: 2 hours	Serves: 8

Ingredients:

- 2.2 lbs. beef, chopped
- 1 lb. onion, chopped
- 1 medium-size pineapple, chopped
- 2 tbsps. vegetable oil
- 2 tbsps. butter
- 1 chili
- Curry powder to taste
- Salt and pepper to taste
- Water as needed

Directions:

1. Chop the meat and drizzle with oil. Season with salt, pepper, and curry powder.
2. Heat the butter and oil in the Dutch oven. Add the meat and fry it for 5 minutes. Then add the onions and chili pieces and cook for 5 minutes.
3. Add the pineapple cubes and water to the Dutch oven and simmer for 2 hours with the lid closed. Stir constantly to prevent curry from burning and add more water if necessary.

Dutch Oven Beef Steak Stew

Cook time: 1 hour and 30 minutes	Serves: 6

Ingredients:

- 2 lbs. sirloin or round steak, cut into thick strips
- 4 large potatoes, peeled and cubed
- 2 sticks celery, chopped
- 2 large carrots, sliced
- 2 cups tomato juice
- 1 tsp sugar
- 4 tbsps. tapioca starch
- Salt and pepper to taste

Directions:

1. Heat oil in the Dutch oven.
2. Add the steak and sear 1 minute per side. Remove the steak and set aside.
3. Add the onion, potatoes, celery, and carrots to the Dutch oven and sauté for 5 minutes.
4. Add the tomato juice, sugar, tapioca starch, salt, and pepper to taste. Place the steak back in the pot.
5. Cover and bake in the oven at 350F for 1 hour and 20 minutes.
6. Serve.

Dutch Oven Beef Broccoli Stew

Cook time: 1 hour and 30 minutes	Serves: 6

Ingredients:

- 2 lbs. beef, boneless, cut into strips
- 4 cups broccoli florets, diced
- ½ cup of soy sauce
- 1 tsp paprika
- 2 onions, diced
- 2 green chilies
- Salt and pepper to taste
- 1 tsp cumin
- 6 cups of water
- 6 garlic cloves, chopped

Directions:

1. In the Dutch oven, place the beef, water, soy sauce, paprika, cumin, garlic, onion, and cover.
2. Cook for 1 hour. Add the broccoli, salt, pepper, and cook for 30 minutes more.
3. Serve.

Chapter 8 Chicken, Duck and Turkey

Chicken in Tomato Gravy

Cook time: 40 minutes	Serves: 5

Ingredients:

- ½ cup of mushrooms, sliced
- 5 chicken breasts
- 2 cups tomatoes, diced
- 2 red bell peppers, sliced
- 1 tbsp thyme
- 1 tbsp parsley
- 2 tbsps. butter
- 1/2 tsp dried sage
- 4 cups chicken stock
- Salt and pepper to taste
- 1/2 tsp paprika
- 1 tsp garlic powder

Directions:

1. Melt the butter in the Dutch oven.
2. Sear the chicken for 3 minutes.
3. Add the tomatoes and stock. Cook on High heat for 20 minutes.
4. Add the rest of the ingredients and cover.
5. Cook for 20 minutes and serve.

Creamy Chicken Breasts and Vegetables

Cook time: 30 minutes	Serves: 4

Ingredients:

- 4 chicken breasts
- 2 cups potatoes, halved
- 1 cup carrot, diced
- 4 red chilies
- 4 cups of coconut milk
- 1 tbsp parsley, chopped
- 1 tbsp coriander, chopped
- Salt and pepper to taste
- 2 tbsps. butter
- 1/2 tsp paprika
- 1 tsp ginger powder
- 1 tsp garlic powder

Directions:

1. In a Dutch oven, add the butter, chicken, potatoes, carrots, and red chilies.
2. Add the ginger, garlic, paprika, salt, pepper, coriander, parsley, and pour in the milk.
3. Cover and cook for 30 minutes.
4. Serve.

Chicken Bean Chili

Cook time: 1 hour	Serves: 6

Ingredients:

- ½ cup sweet corn
- 1 cup kidney beans, boiled
- 6 cups chicken stock
- 1 cup tomatoes, chopped
- 4 chicken breasts, boneless
- 1/2 cup onion, diced
- 4 garlic cloves, sliced
- 1/2 cup celery, chopped
- 1 cup potatoes, chopped
- 1 cup carrot, chopped
- Salt and pepper to taste
- 2 tsps. paprika
- 2 tbsps. ginger powder
- 1 tbsp chives, chopped
- 1 tbsp parsley, chopped
- 1 tbsp mixed herbs
- 1 tbsp soy sauce
- 1 tbsp white vinegar

Directions:

1. In the Dutch oven, add the chicken stock with garlic, ginger, onion, and chicken breasts.
2. Cover and cook for 30 minutes. Shred the chicken.
3. Add the rest of the ingredients and cover.
4. Cook for 30 minutes. Serve.

Duck Carrot Noodle Soup

Cook time: 50 minutes	Serves: 4

Ingredients:

- 1 cup carrot, cubed
- 1 cup onion, cubed
- 2 cups noodles
- 2 duck breasts
- 6 cups vegetable stock
- Salt and pepper to taste
- 1/2 tsp paprika
- 1 tsp garlic powder
- 1 tbsp lemongrass, chopped
- 1 tsp butter
- 1 tsp dried oregano

Directions:

1. Melt the butter in the Dutch oven and cook the duck for 2 minutes.
2. Pour in the vegetable stock, lemongrass, garlic, paprika, and cover.
3. Cook for 30 minutes.
4. Shred the duck breasts and add the carrots. Add the onion, noodles, salt, pepper, and cook for 20 minutes.
5. Serve.

Chicken and White Bean Chili

Cook time: 30 minutes	Serves: 4

Ingredients:

- 2 tbsps. vegetable oil
- ⅔ cup corn kernels
- ½ small onion, chopped
- 1 jalapeño, seeded and minced
- 1 tsp. salt, divided
- 1 cup low-sodium chicken stock
- 1 tbsp. chili powder
- 1 tsp. ground cumin
- ¼ tsp. ground cayenne
- 1-pound boneless skinless chicken breast, cut into 1-inch cubes
- 2 (15-ounce) cans cannellini beans, drained
- 1 (4-ounce) can diced green chiles
- ¼ cup sour cream
- ¼ cup chopped fresh cilantro leaves

Directions:

1. Heat the oil in a Dutch oven until simmering.
2. Add the corn in a single layer and cook without stirring for 4 minutes or until the corn starts to char.
3. Add the jalapeno, onion, and ¼ tsp. of the salt and cook for 3 minutes, or until the onions start to brown.
4. Add the stock and deglaze the pot.

5. Stir in the chili powder, cumin, remaining ¾ tsp. salt and cayenne.
6. Bring to a simmer and add the beans, chicken, and green chilies and their juices.
7. Cover and cook for 15 minutes or until the chicken is cooked.

Moroccan Chicken and Sweet Potatoes

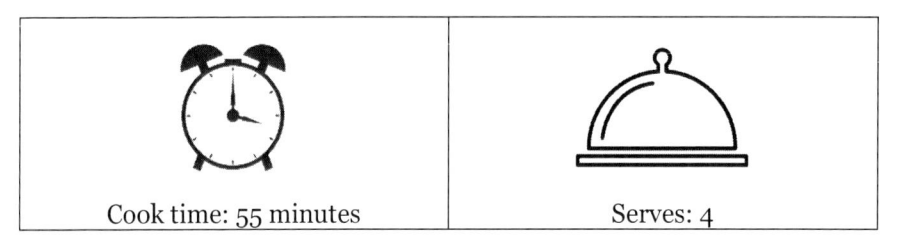

Cook time: 55 minutes	Serves: 4

Ingredients:

- 4 large bone-in, skin-on chicken thighs (6 to 7 ounces each)
- 1¼ tsps. kosher salt, divided
- 1 tbsp. olive oil
- 1 small onion, sliced
- 2 garlic cloves, minced
- 1 tbsp. ground cumin
- 2 tsps. ground coriander
- ½ cup dry white wine
- 1 cup low-sodium chicken stock
- 1 tbsp. orange juice concentrate
- 1-pound sweet potatoes, peeled and cut into ¼-inch-thick slices
- 1 large orange, membrane removed
- ½ cup coarsely chopped Kalamata olives

Directions:

1. Preheat the oven to 300F. Sprinkle the chicken with 1 tsp. salt.
2. In a Dutch oven, heat the oil. Cook the chicken, skin-side down, for 5 to 6 minutes. Flip and cook for 5 minutes more or until browned. Set aside.
3. Cook the onion in the pot for 4 minutes, or until slightly browned.
4. Add the garlic, cumin, and coriander and cook for 1 minute.
5. Add the wine and deglaze the pot. Cook until reduced by half.
6. Add the stock, orange juice, and remaining ¼ tsp. salt. Bring it to a simmer.
7. Add the sweet potatoes in an even layer and place the chicken on top, skin-side up. Cover and bake for 20 minutes.
8. Meanwhile, cut the orange segments from the membranes.
9. Remove the pot from the oven and raise the temperature to 400F.
10. Remove the chicken and set aside. Cut off any fat and gently stir the sweet potatoes. Add the orange segments and juices from the bowl and the olives. Return the chicken to the pot, skin-side up.
11. Bake for 15 to 20 minutes, uncovered, or until the chicken skin is crisp.
12. Serve.

Duck with Olive Sauce

Cook time: 1 hour and 30 minutes	Serves: 6

Ingredients:

- 1 tbsp. extra-virgin olive oil
- 6 duck breasts, skin scored
- 3 shallots, minced
- 2 garlic cloves
- 1 tbsp. roughly chopped fresh thyme leaves
- 1 bay leaf
- 1½ cups dry white wine
- Black pepper to taste
- ½ cup pitted Kalamata olives
- 1 bouillon cube
- 1 cup of water

Directions:

1. Preheat the oven to 300F.
2. Heat the oil in the Dutch oven.
3. Lower heat and sear the duck breasts, skin-side down, until crisp. Remove to a plate.
4. Strain the fat from the pot. Add the garlic and shallots. Brown lightly. Add the bay leaf and thyme and sauté for 1 minute.
5. Add the wine, season with pepper, and reduce by half. Add the olives and sauté for 1 minute.
6. Return the duck breasts to the pot, skin-side up. Add the water and bouillon cube and bring to a boil.

7. Cover, and place in the preheated oven.
8. Cook for 30 to 45 minutes or until the duck breast is tender.
9. Remove the duck breasts and place them on a platter. Reduce the sauce, skimming the fat from the top. Serve.

Wild Duck Gumbo Stew

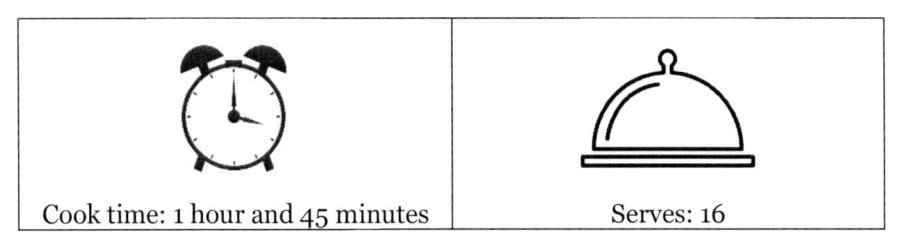

Cook time: 1 hour and 45 minutes	Serves: 16

Cook time: 1 hour 45 minutes |Serves: 16|

Ingredients:

- 2 wild ducks, chopped up
- ½ cup oil
- ⅔ cup all-purpose flour
- 1-lb. smoked sausage, sliced
- 2 cups, onion, peeled and chopped
- 1½ cups, green pepper, chopped
- 1½ cups, celery, sliced
- 2 tbsps. fresh parsley, minced
- 1 tbsp. garlic, peeled and minced
- 1 (15-oz) can stewed tomatoes
- 2 bay leaves
- 2 tbsps. Worcestershire sauce
- 1½ tsps. pepper
- 1 tsp. salt
- 1 tsp. dried thyme
- ¼ tsp. cayenne pepper

- 4 cups of water

Directions:

1. Heat the oil in the Dutch oven. Brown the duck in the pot in batches. Transfer the duck to a plate and discard all the fat apart from 2/3 cup.
2. Add the flour to the 2/3 cup of drippings and cook and stir until brown, about 12 to 15 minutes.
3. Next, add the sausage, onion, green pepper, celery, parsley, and garlic. Cook for 10 minutes.
4. Stir in the tomatoes, bay leaves, Worcestershire sauce, pepper, salt, dried thyme, cayenne pepper, and water.
5. Add the browned duck and bring it to a boil.
6. Turn the heat down, cover, and simmer for 1 to 1 ¼ hour or until the meat is tender.
7. Remove the duck and allow it to cool before cutting into chunks.
8. Return the chunks of meat to the pan and heat through on simmer for 5 to 10 minutes.
9. Remove and discard the bay leaves and serve.

Duck and Sausage Cassoulet

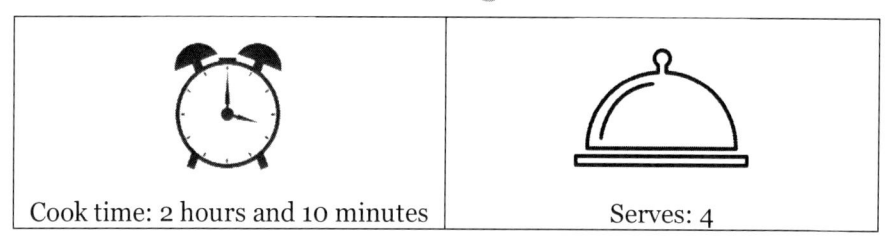

Cook time: 2 hours and 10 minutes	Serves: 4

Ingredients:

For the Stew

- ½ pound bacon, diced
- 4 duck legs
- Salt and pepper to taste

- 4 uncooked sausages
- 1 large onion, diced
- 3 garlic cloves, minced
- 1 celery stalk, chopped
- 1 tbsp. tomato paste
- 1 (14.5-oz) can stewed tomatoes, puréed or finely chopped
- 1-pound dried white beans, soaked for at least 8 hours, and then drained
- 3 fresh thyme sprigs
- 3 flat-leaf parsley sprigs
- 1 bay leaf
- 3 whole cloves
- ¼ tsp. whole black peppercorns

For the breadcrumb topping

- 2 cups coarse fresh breadcrumbs
- 2 garlic cloves, minced
- ½ cup minced flat-leaf parsley
- 1½ tsps. kosher salt
- ½ tsp. freshly ground black pepper
- 6 tbsps. unsalted butter, melted

Directions:

1. To make the stew: preheat the oven to 400F.
2. Cook the bacon in the Dutch oven for 4 minutes. Then transfer to a paper-towel-lined plate.
3. Season the duck legs with salt and pepper. Add the duck legs to the Dutch oven and cook until well browned on both sides, about 5 minutes per side. Transfer the duck legs to the plate with the bacon. Drain and reserve most of the fat from the pot.

4. Add the sausages to the Dutch oven and cook until browned on all sides, about 6 minutes. Transfer the sausages to the plate with the duck and bacon. Again, drain most of the fat from the pot and leave about 2 tbsps. for sautéing the vegetables.
5. Add the onion, garlic, and celery to the pot and cook for 10 minutes, or until beginning to brown.
6. Stir in the tomato paste and cook for 2 minutes more. Add the tomatoes and beans and enough water to cover the beans completely. Bring to a boil. Add the browned bacon and stir to mix well. Place the duck legs and sausages in the pot.
7. Wrap the thyme and parsley sprigs, the bay leaf, cloves, and peppercorns in a piece of cheesecloth and tie with a piece of kitchen twine. Tuck this bundle into the Dutch oven.
8. Cover the pot and bake for 1 ½ hour, until the beans are tender and duck legs are cooked.
9. To make the breadcrumb topping: In a bowl, stir together the breadcrumbs, garlic, parsley, salt, pepper, and melted butter.
10. Remove the Dutch oven from the oven and lower heat to 350F. Remove the herb bundle from the stew and discard it. Spread the bread crumb mixture evenly over the top of the stew and return the pot to the oven.
11. Cook, uncovered, for 10 minutes. Serve.

Turkey, Bean & Corn Chili

Cook time: 1 hour and 30 minutes	Serves: 8

Ingredients:

- 1 tbsp. vegetable oil
- 2 strips bacon, diced
- 1 onion, chopped
- 1 red bell pepper, diced
- 3 garlic cloves, chopped
- 1½ pounds ground turkey
- ¼ cup chili powder
- 2 tsps. ground cumin
- 2 tsps. dried oregano
- Salt and black pepper
- 1 (15-ounce) can crushed tomatoes
- 1 ½ cups low-sodium chicken broth
- 1 (15-ounce) can pinto beans, drained and rinsed
- 1 (15-ounce) can sweet corn

Directions:

1. Heat the oil in a Dutch oven. Add the bacon and cook until crispy.
2. Add the onion and red pepper. Cook for 5 minutes. Add the garlic and cook for 2 minutes more.
3. Add the ground turkey and cook for 5 minutes or no longer pink.
4. Stir in the chili powder, cumin, and oregano. Season with salt and pepper.

5. Stir in the tomatoes, and broth. Bring the mixture to a boil and lower heat to simmer.
6. Simmer, uncovered, for 45 minutes to 1 hour. Stirring occasionally.
7. Fold in the corn and pinto beans. Simmer for 15 minutes.
8. Serve.

Mexican Turkey Soup

Cook time: 40 minutes	Serves: 6

Ingredients:

- Cooking spray
- 1 cup onion, chopped
- 1 red sweet pepper, chopped
- ½ tsp. paprika
- 1 tsp. chili powder
- 1 tsp. ground cumin
- 5 cups low-sodium chicken broth
- 1 tomato, chopped
- 1 ½ cups winter squash, sliced into cubes
- Salt and pepper to taste
- 2 cups turkey, cooked and shredded
- 2 tbsps. cilantro, chopped
- 1 cup corn kernels

Directions:

1. Spray the Dutch oven with oil and heat over medium heat.

2. Cook the onion and sweet pepper for 5 minutes.
3. Season with paprika, chili powder, and cumin.
4. Cook for 30 seconds and stir in the broth.
5. Add tomato and squash. Season with salt and pepper.
6. Bring to a boil and lower heat.
7. Cover and simmer for 20 minutes.
8. Add the cooked turkey, cilantro, and corn.
9. Serve warm.

Turkey Meatballs in Cranberry Sauce

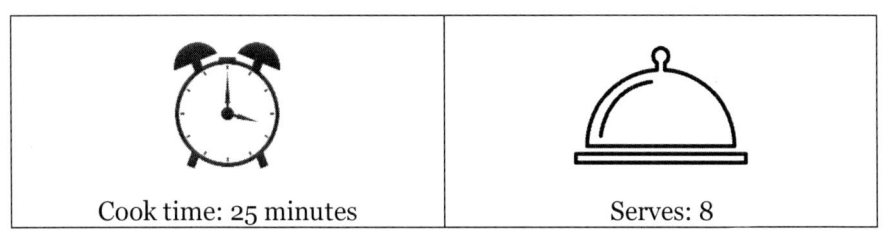

Cook time: 25 minutes	Serves: 8

Ingredients:

- 1 (2-lbs) package frozen prepared turkey meatballs
- 1 (6-oz) bottle mild chili sauce
- 1 (16-oz.) can cranberry jelly sauce
- 2 tbsps. brown sugar
- 1 tbsp. lemon juice

Directions:

1. In the Dutch oven, combine everything except for the meatballs.
2. Cook until the sugar dissolves.
3. Add the meatballs and cook for 20 to 25 minutes.
4. Serve.

Turkey Shepherd's Pie

Cook time: 1 hour and 15 minutes	Serves: 8

Ingredients:

- 2½ pounds sweet potatoes, peeled and cut into cubes
- Salt to taste
- 4 tbsps. butter, divided
- 3 carrots, peeled and diced
- 2 celery stalks, diced
- 1 onion, diced
- 2 tbsps. chopped fresh thyme
- 2 pounds turkey, cooked and chopped
- ¼ cup tomato paste
- 2 tbsps. all-purpose flour
- 2 tbsps. Worcestershire sauce
- 2 cups chicken broth
- ½ cup heavy cream
- Black pepper to taste

Directions:

1. Preheat the oven to 375F.
2. Place the sweet potatoes in a saucepan and cover with water. Add salt and bring to a simmer. Lower heat and simmer for 20 minutes or until the potatoes are tender.
3. Meanwhile, melt 2 tbsps. butter in the Dutch oven. Add the carrots, celery, and onion and cook for 12 minutes.

4. Stir in the thyme, turkey, tomato paste, flour, and sauce. Add the broth and bring to a simmer. Cook for 5 minutes or until the sauce thickens.
5. Drain the potatoes and transfer to a bowl. Add the remaining 2 tbsps. butter, cream, and season with salt and pepper. Mash the potatoes and mix well.
6. Spread the turkey mixture in the Dutch oven in an even layer and top with the mashed potato mixture.
7. Transfer to the oven and bake for 35 minutes, or until the top is lightly browned. Serve hot.

Braised Turkey Legs and Apples

Cook time: 4 hours	Serves: 8

Ingredients:

- 2 skin-on and bone-in turkey drumsticks
- 2 skin-on turkey thighs
- 6 cups chicken broth
- 2 green apples, peeled and cut into quarters
- 8 baby carrots, peeled
- 1 medium white onion, chopped
- 2 large leeks, sliced
- 2 cloves of garlic, minced
- 1 ½ cups dry white wine
- 4 sprigs thyme
- 2 tbsp vegetable oil

Directions:

1. Season the turkey pieces with salt and water. Heat oil in a Dutch oven.
2. Sear the turkey on all sides, around 4 minutes per side. Take off the pot.
3. Add the onion, leeks, garlic, and sauté for 8 to 10 minutes. Add the white wine and thyme and bring to a boil until reduced by 70%.
4. Return the turkey to the pot and add the chicken broth. Bring to a boil and lower the heat. Simmer for 3 hours.
5. Add carrots, and cook uncovered until meat is falling off the bone, about 35 to 45 minutes later. Season with salt and pepper.
6. Strain the sauce and serve.

Turkey Curry

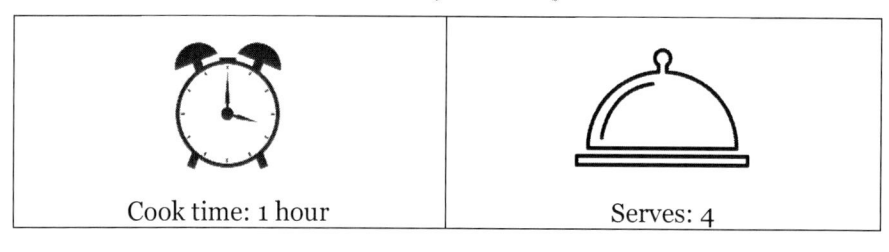

Cook time: 1 hour	Serves: 4

Ingredients:

- 2 lbs. of turkey breast, chopped into cubes of about ½ inch each
- 2 cups of coconut milk
- 2 cups cauliflower florets
- 1 and ½ cups of tomato puree
- 1 and ½ cups of onion small diced
- 3 tbsps. olive oil
- 2 tbsps. chopped cilantro
- 1 tbsp. jalapeno minced
- 1 tbsp. minced garlic
- 1 tbsp. minced ginger

- 4 tsps. yellow curry paste
- 1 and ¼ tsps. ground turmeric
- ¼ tsp. ground coriander
- Salt to taste

Directions:

1. Heat the oil in the Dutch oven on medium heat.
2. Preheat the oven to 400F.
3. Season the turkey with salt and cook in the Dutch oven in batches (5 minutes per batch). Transfer turkey to a plate.
4. Add the garlic, ginger, jalapeno, coriander, 1 tsp. turmeric, and the curry paste and cook for 3 minutes.
5. Put in the onion and cook for 5 minutes. Then pour in the tomato puree and coconut milk. Allow the mixture to come to a boil.
6. Return the turkey to the Dutch oven and lower heat to simmer. Then slightly cover and cook for 30 minutes.
7. Meanwhile, toss the cauliflower in the remaining olive oil. Then add the turmeric and season with salt.
8. Place the cauliflower on a baking sheet and roast at 400F for 15 minutes.
9. When the turkey is cooked, stir in the cauliflower and adjust seasoning.
10. Garnish with cilantro and serve.

Chapter 9 Pork and Lamb

Noodles with Pork

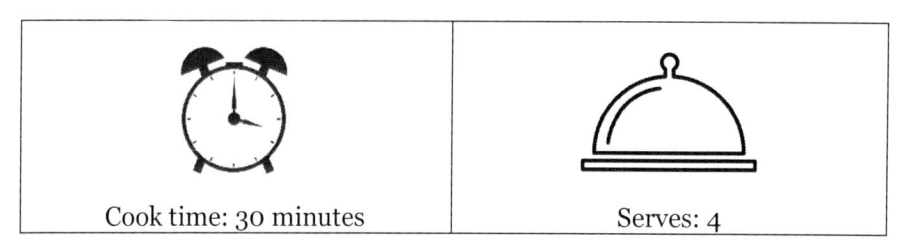

Cook time: 30 minutes	Serves: 4

Ingredients:

- 1 tbsp. salt
- 3 tbsps. soy sauce
- 2 tbsps. peanut butter
- 6 tsps. toasted sesame oil, divided
- 1 tbsp. rice vinegar
- 1 tsp. red pepper flakes
- ½ English cucumber, chopped
- 8 ounces Chinese wheat noodles
- 1 tbsp. vegetable oil
- 1-pound ground pork
- 2 tsps. minced fresh ginger
- 2 tsps. minced garlic
- ⅓ cup coarsely chopped roasted salted peanuts
- 2 scallions, both white and green parts, sliced

Directions:

1. Bring 2 quarts of water and the salt to a boil in the Dutch oven.

2. Meanwhile, in a bowl, stir together the soy sauce, peanut butter, 4 tsps. sesame oil, rice vinegar, and red pepper flakes.
3. Add the noodles to the boiling water and cook according to package directions. Then rinse with cool water and drain. Toss with the remaining 2 tsps. of sesame oil.
4. Clean the Dutch oven and heat the oil until simmering.
5. Add the pork and cook for 4 minutes. Add the ginger and garlic and cook until the pork is browned.
6. Add the noodles and sauce and mix. Stir in the cucumbers.
7. Top with the peanuts and scallions and serve.

Pork Piccata

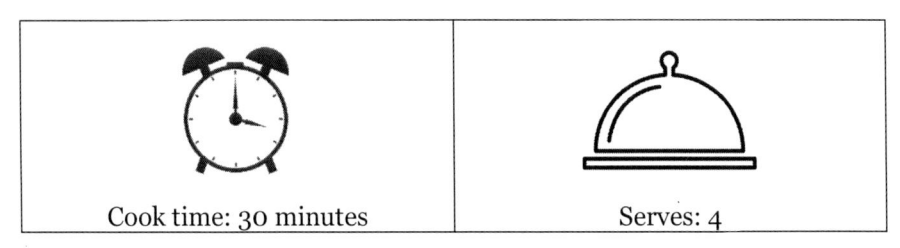

Cook time: 30 minutes	Serves: 4

Ingredients:

- 1 (1¼-pounds) pork tenderloin, sliced into 1 ½ inch thick medallions
- 1½ tsps. salt, divided
- ½ cup flour
- 6 tbsps. unsalted butter, divided
- ¼ cup lemon juice
- ¼ cup low-sodium chicken stock
- 3 tbsps. capers
- 3 tbsps. chopped fresh parsley

Directions:

1. Cover the pork slices with a plastic wrap and flatten the medallions with a mallet to about ¼ inch. Season with 1 tsp. salt and then dredge lightly with flour.
2. Heat 4 tbsps. butter in the Dutch oven and cook the pork (in batches) until browned. Transfer pork to a plate.
3. Add the lemon juice, chicken stock, and capers to the pot. Bring to a boil and deglaze. Cook until reduced by half.
4. Remove the Dutch oven from the heat and cook for 2 minutes. 1 tbsp. at a time, swirl in the remaining 2 tbsps. of the butter to thicken the sauce. Stir in the parsley.
5. Add the pork medallions and coat with the sauce.
6. Serve.

Pork Medallions with Mustard Sauce

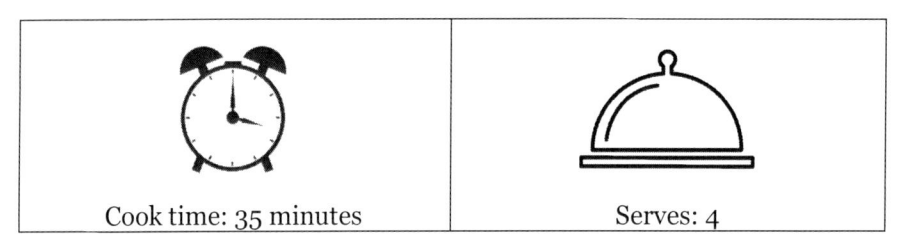

Cook time: 35 minutes	Serves: 4

Ingredients:

- 1 (1¼-pounds) pork tenderloin, sliced into 1 ½ inch thick medallions
- 2 tsps. salt, divided
- ½ tsp. black pepper, divided
- 3 tbsps. vegetable oil, divided
- 1 tart apple, peeled, cored, and sliced
- ⅔ cup hard apple cider
- ½ cup heavy cream
- 1 tbsp. Dijon mustard

Directions:

1. Flatten the pork medallions to about ¾ inch. Season with 1 tsp. salt and ¼ tsp. black pepper.
2. Heat 2 tbsps. oil in the Dutch oven and cook the pork (in batches) until deep golden brown. Transfer the pork to a plate.
3. Heat the remaining 1 tbsp. oil and add the apple slices. Cook for 5 minutes.
4. Add the cider cook for 3 minutes or until reduced by half.
5. Stir in the cream and mustard and cook for 5 minutes.
6. Return the pork to the pot and coat with the sauce.
7. Sprinkle with salt and pepper and serve.

Chorizo-Stuffed Peppers

Cook time: 1 hour	Serves: 4

Ingredients:

- 4 large bell peppers
- ½ tsp. kosher salt
- 1 tbsp. vegetable oil
- 12 ounces Mexican chorizo, casings removed
- 1½ cups cooked white or brown rice
- ¾ cup diced canned tomatoes, drained
- 1½ cups grated Monterey Jack cheese, divided

Directions:

1. Preheat the oven to 375F.
2. Bring 1 inch of water to a boil in a Dutch oven.

3. Slice ¼ inch off the top of each pepper, reserving the tops. Remove the core and ribs. Remove the stems from the tops and chop the flesh.
4. Steam the peppers (cut-side down) in a steamer basket for 4 minutes. Then sprinkle the insides with the salt.
5. Heat the oil in the Dutch oven. Cook the chorizo for 5 minutes, or until mostly browned.
6. Add the chopped peppers and cook for 4 minutes.
7. In a bowl, combine the chorizo mixture, rice, and tomatoes. Mix and stir in 1 cup of the cheese.
8. Spoon the mixture into the peppers. Top with the remaining ½ cup of cheese.
9. Place the peppers in the Dutch oven and cover. Bake for 25 minutes.
10. Remove the lid and cook for another 15 minutes.
11. Serve.

Pork Chili Verde with Rice

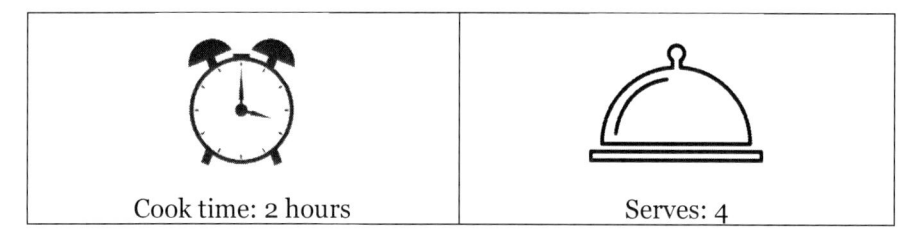

Cook time: 2 hours	Serves: 4

Ingredients:

- 2 pounds boneless pork shoulder, cut into 3-inch strips
- 1½ tsps. salt, divided
- 1 tbsp. vegetable oil
- 1 cup tomatillo salsa
- ½ cup low-sodium chicken stock
- 1 poblano chile, seeded and chopped
- 1 cup long-grain white rice
- ¼ cup chopped fresh cilantro

Directions:

1. Season the pork with 1 tsp. salt.
2. Heat the oil in the Dutch oven. Brown the pork for 4 minutes.
3. Flip the pieces and add the salsa, stock, and poblano and stir.
4. Preheat the oven to 250F. Transfer the Dutch oven to the oven with the lid ajar. Cook for 1 hour.
5. Now increase the heat to 300F and remove the lid. Cook for 30 to 50 minutes more or until the pork is tender.
6. Remove the pot from the oven. Transfer the pork to a cutting board. Skim off the fat from the sauce. You should get about 2 cups of sauce. If less, then add salsa to make 2 cups. Return the sauce to the pot and add the rice and remaining ½ tsp. salt.
7. Bring to a boil and lower heat. Cover and cook for 20 minutes.
8. Meanwhile, pull the pork into bite-size chunks.
9. The rice should be done after 20 minutes.
10. Stir in the pork and cilantro. Warm for 3 minutes and serve.

Pork Ribs Cacciatore

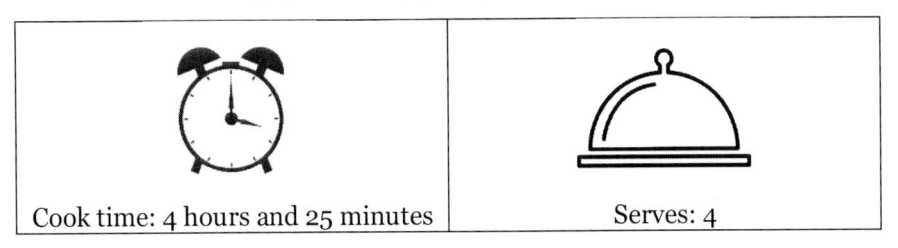

Cook time: 4 hours and 25 minutes	Serves: 4

Ingredients:

- 1 rack pork back ribs, cut into 2-rib sections
- 2 tsps. kosher salt, divided
- 2 tbsps. olive oil
- 1½ cups sliced cremini mushrooms

- 1 small onion, sliced
- 2 garlic cloves, minced
- ½ cup dry red wine
- 1 (14.5-ounce) can diced tomatoes
- 1 cup low-sodium chicken stock
- 1 tsp. dried oregano
- 2 tbsps. chopped fresh parsley
- 2 tbsps. capers

Directions:

1. Season the ribs with 1 tsp. salt.
2. Heat the oil in a Dutch oven.
3. Add the ribs and brown on one side for 4 to 5 minutes. Transfer to a plate.
4. Add the onion, mushrooms, garlic, and remaining 1 tsp. salt to the pot. Cook for 3 minutes.
5. Add the wine and deglaze the pot. Boil until reduced by half. Add the tomatoes and their juices, stock, and oregano.
6. Preheat the oven to 200F. Transfer the pot to the oven with the lid ajar.
7. Cook for 1 hour, then increase the heat to 250F. cook for 1 hour and 30 minutes. Increase the temperature to 300F and cook for 1 hour to 1 hour 30 minutes or until the ribs are very tender.
8. Remove the ribs from the pot and remove as much fat as possible from the sauce.
9. Return the ribs to the pot. Stir in the parsley and capers. Serve.

Stuffed Bacon-Wrapped Pork Tenderloin

Cook time: 55 minutes	Serves: 4

Ingredients:

- 1 (1½ pounds) pork tenderloin
- 1½ tsps. salt, divided
- ½ cup apple cider
- 2 tbsps. cider vinegar
- ¾ cup dried cherries
- 1 tbsp. vegetable oil
- 1 shallot, minced
- 1 garlic clove, minced
- ½ cup fresh breadcrumbs
- 1 tsp. dried thyme
- 4 to 6 slices bacon or prosciutto

Directions:

1. Preheat the oven to 375F.
2. Season the pork with 1 tsp. salt.
3. Bring the apple cider and vinegar to a simmer in a small pot. Add the cherries and set aside to rehydrate.
4. Heat the oil in the Dutch oven. Add the shallot and garlic and cook for 2 minutes.
5. Add the breadcrumbs, thyme, and remaining ½ tsp. salt. Mix.
6. Pour in the cherries and liquid into the pot and stir.
7. Cut the tenderloin lengthwise to about ½ inch from the side. Spread the cherry stuffing over half of the

tenderloin and fold the other half over. Wrap the tenderloin with strips of bacon, securing the bacon with toothpicks. Cut the tenderloin in half, so it fits in the Dutch oven.
8. Place the pot in the oven, uncovered, and roast for 15 minutes. Remove the pot and turn the pork over.
9. Roast for another 12 to 15 minutes or until pork reaches 140F to 145F.
10. Remove toothpicks. Serve.

Lamb Shanks with White Beans

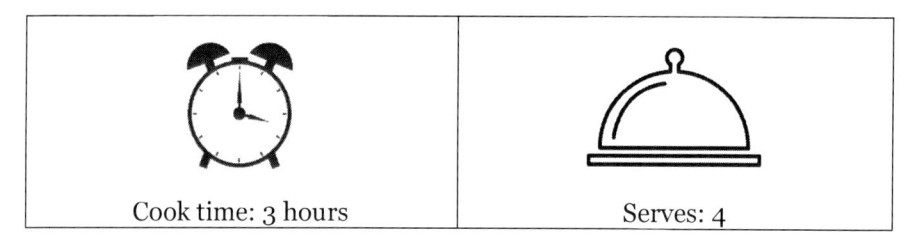

Cook time: 3 hours	Serves: 4

Ingredients:

- 4 pounds lamb shanks (4 to 6 shanks)
- 3 tsps. salt, divided
- 2 tbsps. olive oil
- ½ cup dry white wine
- 2 cups low-sodium chicken stock
- 1⅔ cups dry cannellini or white northern beans
- 1 (14.5-ounce) can diced tomatoes
- 1 medium onion, quartered
- 2 garlic cloves, peeled
- 1 bay leaf
- ½ tsp. black pepper
- 1 cup pitted green olives
- ¼ cup chopped parsley

Directions:

1. Preheat the oven to 325F.
2. Sprinkle the lamb with 2 tsps. salt.
3. Heat the oil in a Dutch oven. Add the lamb and brown for 4 minutes. Transfer the lamb to a cutting board.
4. Add the wine to the pot and bring to a simmer. Deglaze the pot. Let the wine reduce by half.
5. Add the lamb shanks, stock, beans, tomatoes, and their juices, onion, garlic, bay leaf, remaining 1 tsp. salt, and black pepper. Bring it to a simmer.
6. Cover the pot and cook in the oven for an hour. Then set the lid ajar and cook for 30 minutes to 1 hour more.
7. Remove the bay leaf, garnish with olives and parsley. Serve.

Roasted Rack of Lamb and Baby Potatoes

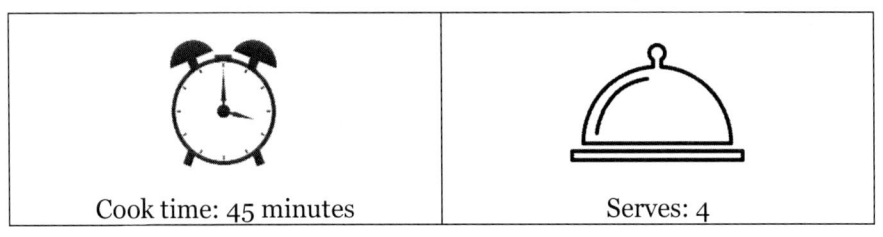

Cook time: 45 minutes	Serves: 4

Ingredients:

- 2 (1¼ pounds) racks of lamb, frenched
- 1½ tsps. kosher salt, divided
- 3 tbsps. vegetable oil, divided
- 12 ounces baby potatoes
- 1 garlic head, plus 1 large-peeled garlic clove, divided
- 2 English muffins, torn into 1-inch pieces
- ¼ cup fresh parsley leaves
- ½ tsp. grated lemon zest
- ¼ tsp. black pepper
- 1 tsp. unsalted butter, melted
- 2 tsps. Dijon-style mustard

Directions:

1. Preheat the oven to 375F. Season the lamb with 1 tsp. salt.
2. Heat 1 ½ tbsps. oil in the Dutch oven. Place one lamb rack in the pot, meat-side down. Sear for 2 minutes. Turn the rack to sear the ends. Repeat with the other rack and set the racks aside.
3. Cut the head of the garlic in half. Place in the pot along with the potatoes.
4. Drizzle with the remaining 1 ½ tbsps. oil and ½ tsp. salt. Mix.
5. Place in the oven, uncovered, and cook for 20 minutes.
6. In a food processor, mince the remaining garlic clove. Add the English muffin and parsley and process into coarse crumbs. Add the lemon zest, black pepper, and butter and pulse to make persillade.
7. Brush the meat side of each rack with mustard. Press the persillade over the meat.
8. Remove the pot from the oven. Toss the potatoes and place the lamb rack on top.
9. Roast for 20 to 25 minutes, or until meat reaches 125F.
10. Remove and let rest until the internal temperature has reached 135F.

Lamb Tomato Zucchini Stew

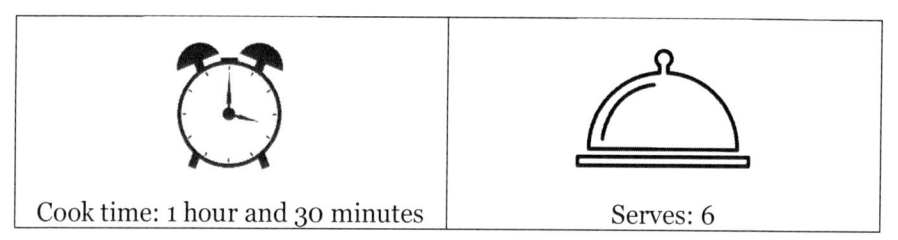

Cook time: 1 hour and 30 minutes	Serves: 6

Ingredients:

- ½ cup peas
- 2 lbs. lamb meat, cut into medium chunks
- 2 cups tomatoes, halved

- 2 cups zucchini, cut into large chunks
- 1 tsp cumin
- 1 tsp paprika
- 1 tbsp honey
- Salt and pepper to taste
- 6 cups of water
- 1 tsp ginger powder
- 1 tsp garlic powder

Directions:

1. In a Dutch oven, add the lamb meat with water. Add the garlic, ginger, honey, paprika, cumin, and mix well. Cover and cook for 1 hour.
2. Add the peas, zucchini, tomatoes, salt, and pepper and cook for 30 minutes.
3. Serve.

Greek Lamb Stew with Orzo

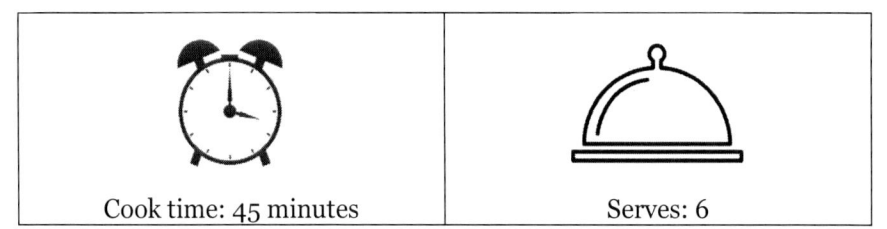

Cook time: 45 minutes	Serves: 6

Ingredients:

- 2 lbs. lamb chunks (for stew)
- 1 ½ cups orzo pasta
- 1 large white onion, chopped
- ½ cup red wine
- 2 tbsps. tomato paste
- 1 (14 oz.) can chopped tomatoes
- 3 ½ cups vegetable broth

- 1 tsp cinnamon
- ½ tsp nutmeg
- 1 tsp sugar
- ½ cup feta or kefalotyri cheese
- Salt and pepper to taste

Directions:

1. Warm half of the oil in a Dutch oven and sear the meat on all sides to brown. Work in batches. Remove the meat to a plate.
2. Add the remaining oil to the pot and cook onions until transparent, about 5 minutes. Add the garlic and cook for 1 minute more.
3. Deglaze the pot with red wine and cook until reduced by half.
4. Add the meat back with the remaining ingredients.
5. Cover the lid and cook at 350F for 1 hour.
6. Serve with feta on top.

Lamb Shanks with Vegetables

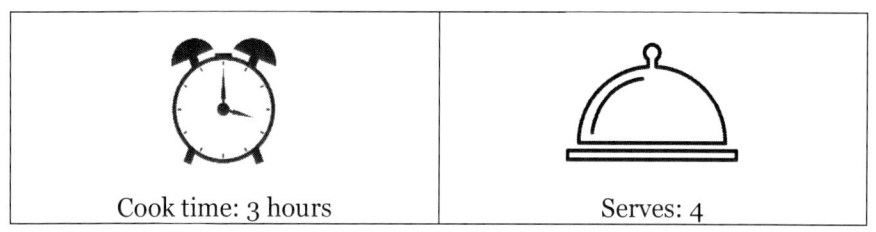

Cook time: 3 hours	Serves: 4

Ingredients:

- 4 lamb shanks
- Salt and pepper to taste
- 2 tbsps. extra-virgin olive oil
- 2 onions, chopped
- 2 carrots, chopped
- 2 parsnips, chopped

- 1 (28-ounce) can whole Italian plum tomatoes
- 1 cup chicken broth or stock
- 1 cup beef broth or stock
- 1 can chickpeas, drained and rinsed
- 1 tsp. dried thyme
- Parsley, for garnish

Directions:

1. Season the lamb shanks with salt and pepper.
2. Heat the olive oil in a Dutch oven. Brown the shanks, two at a time, about 2 minutes per side. Remove to a platter.
3. Add the onions, carrots, and parsnips to the pot. Sauté for 5 to 7 minutes, or until lightly browned.
4. Increase the heat to medium-high. Add the tomatoes, both the broths, chickpeas, and thyme. Bring to a boil.
5. Return the shanks to the pot. Briefly bring to a boil and cover. Lower the heat to low and simmer for 2 ½ hours or until the meat is tender.
6. Remove the lid and increase the heat to medium-high. Cook for 10 minutes.
7. Garnish and serve.

Spanish Lamb Stew

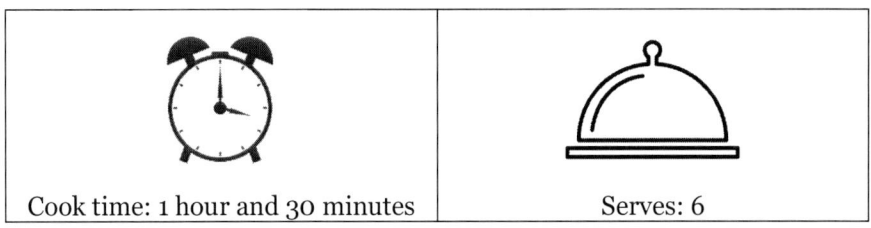

Cook time: 1 hour and 30 minutes	Serves: 6

Ingredients:

- 2 tbsps. extra-virgin olive oil
- 2 pounds lamb stew meat, cut into 1-inch pieces
- 1 yellow onion, minced

- Salt and pepper to taste
- 2 tbsps. all-purpose flour
- 3 cloves garlic, minced
- 1½ cups diced tomatoes
- 1 bay leaf
- 4 cups of water
- 2 pounds fresh shelled beans (cannellini beans, cranberry beans, black-eyed peas, or garbanzo beans), shelled
- ½ pound chorizo, sliced

Directions:

1. Heat the olive oil in the Dutch oven. Add the lamb and onion and season with salt and pepper.
2. Cook for 8 to 10 minutes or until the lamb is golden on all sides. Sprinkle the flour into the pot and stir. Cook for 2 minutes.
3. Add the garlic, tomatoes, bay leaf, and water. Bring to a boil over high heat. Lower the heat to low, and simmer for 1 hour.
4. Add the beans and chorizo and simmer for 40 minutes.
5. Remove the bay leaf and serve.

Shepherd's Pie

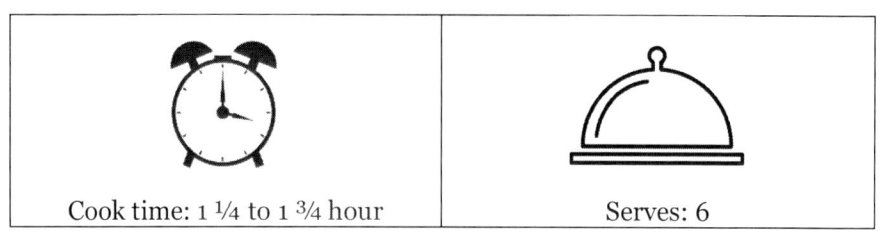

Cook time: 1 ¼ to 1 ¾ hour	Serves: 6

Ingredients:

- 1 (16-ounce) package frozen mixed vegetables
- 2 pounds ground lamb

- 1 cup broth or stock
- 1 tbsp. tomato paste
- 1 tbsp. Worcestershire sauce
- 2 cloves garlic, minced
- 1 tsp. crushed dried thyme
- Salt to taste
- 1 (32-ounce) package refrigerated mashed potatoes

Directions:

1. Preheat the oven to 325F.
2. Place the frozen vegetables in the Dutch oven. Add the broth, ground lamb, tomato paste, Worcestershire sauce, garlic, thyme, salt, and pepper. Mix.
3. Cover and place in the heated oven. Cook for 1 to 1 ½ hours.
4. Remove the pot from the oven and lower the temperature to 350F.
5. Meanwhile, spoon the mashed potatoes into small mounds on top of the meat mixture. Smooth the surface with the back of the spoon.
6. Return the pot to the oven, uncovered, and bake for 15 minutes.
7. Serve.

Lamb Curry

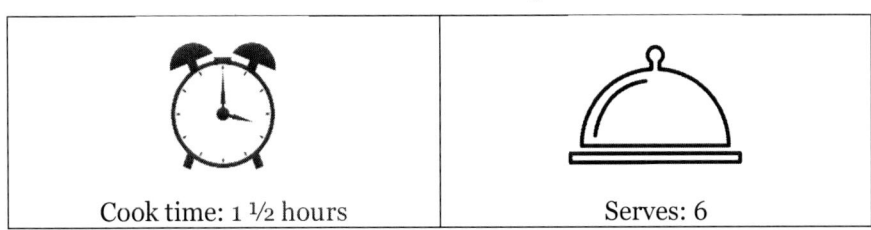

Cook time: 1 ½ hours	Serves: 6

Ingredients:

- 2 tbsps. extra-virgin olive oil

- 3 pounds lamb stew meat, trimmed, and cut into 1-inch cubes
- 2 onions, chopped
- 4 cloves garlic, minced
- 2 tbsps. curry powder
- 1 tsp. ground coriander
- 1 tsp. ground cumin
- Salt and pepper to taste
- 2 cups broth or stock

Directions:

1. Heat the oil in a Dutch oven. Working in batches, cook the lamb pieces until browned on all sides. Then transfer to a plate.
2. Add the onions and garlic and cook until translucent. Reduce the heat to medium. Add curry powder, coriander, cumin, salt, and pepper. Cook for 3 minutes.
3. Return the meat to the pot. Pour in the broth. Bring to a boil and reduce to a simmer. Cook, uncovered, for about 1 ¼ hours.

Chapter 10 Fish and Seafood

Salt-Crusted Citrus Snapper

Cook time: 35 to 40 minutes	Serves: 6

Ingredients:

- 2 pounds of sea salt
- ¾ to 1 cup of water
- Cooking spray
- 1 large orange, sliced, divided
- 1 large lemon, sliced, divided
- 1 large grapefruit, sliced, divided
- 1 (4-pound) whole red snapper, cleaned and scaled

Directions:

1. Preheat the oven to 375F.
2. In a bowl, combine the salt and water. Mix to make a paste.
3. Coat a Dutch oven with cooking spray. Then pour a 1-inch thick layer of the salt mixture into the bottom of the pot. Layer half of the orange, lemon, and grapefruit slices on top of the salt. Place the red snapper on top of the slices. Press the remaining salt on top of the fish to form a thick crust. Top with the remaining fruit slices.
4. Cover and place the oven. Bake for 35 to 40 minutes. Serve.

Spice-Rubbed Salmon

Cook time: 20 minutes	Serves: 4

Ingredients:

- 1 tsp. salt
- 1 tsp. chili powder
- 1 tsp. cumin
- 4 (6-ounce) salmon fillets, skin on
- 1 tbsp. olive oil

Directions:

1. Preheat the oven to 375F.
2. In a bowl, combine the salt, chili powder, and cumin. Rub the salmon fillets with the spice mixture and coat evenly.
3. Heat oil in the Dutch oven. Place the salmon fillets in the pot, skin-side up. Cook for 3 minutes. For medium-rare, flip, and cook for 3 minutes. For medium to well-done, cover, place in the oven, and bake for 5 to 10 minutes.
4. Serve.

Steamed Mussels with Bacon

Cook time: 15 minutes	Serves: 6

Ingredients:

- 3 tbsps. extra-virgin olive oil, plus more for garnish
- ½ cup bacon, diced
- 4 cloves garlic, thinly sliced
- 1 onion, chopped
- 1 cup dry white wine
- 2 tsps. paprika
- 2 dozen mussels, cleaned and beards removed
- Cayenne pepper, for garnish
- Handful fresh oregano, chopped, for garnish

Directions:

1. Heat the oil in the Dutch oven and cook the bacon for 2 minutes.
2. Then add the garlic, and onion. Cook until translucent.
3. Add the wine and stir in the paprika.
4. Add the mussels and increase the heat. Cook for 30 seconds or until the alcohol has evaporated.
5. Lower the heat and cover the pot. Steam for 5 to 8 minutes, or until all the mussels have opened. Discard any mussels that haven't opened.
6. Garnish and serve.

Spanish Paella

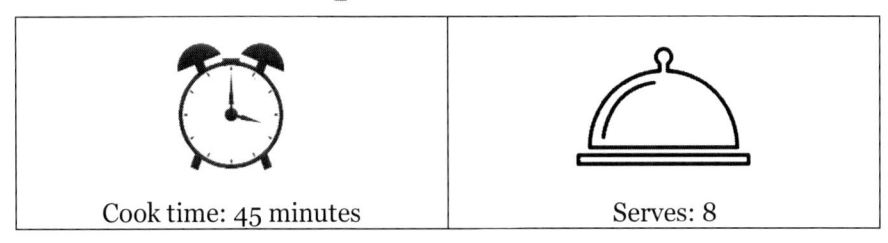

Cook time: 45 minutes	Serves: 8

Ingredients:

- 3 tbsps. extra-virgin olive oil

- 2 pounds chicken thighs, skinned, boned, and cut into 2-inch pieces
- 5½ cups low-sodium chicken broth or stock
- ½ pound shrimp, peeled and shells reserved
- 1½ pounds paella rice, or any Spanish-style medium-grain rice
- ¼ tsp. saffron or turmeric
- 1 (15-ounce) can cannellini beans, drained and rinsed
- ¾ pound tomatoes, peeled, halved, seeded, and finely chopped
- 1 tbsp. smoked paprika
- 1 dozen mussels, scrubbed
- Sea salt to taste

Directions:

1. Heat the olive oil in the Dutch oven. Add the chicken and sauté until golden. Transfer the chicken to a plate. Pour off the fat from the pot.
2. Return the pot to the heat. Add the broth and bring to a boil. Add the shrimp shells (reserving the shrimp), and simmer for 15 to 20 minutes. Remove the shells and discard.
3. Stir in the rice and cook for 10 minutes.
4. Add the chicken, saffron, beans, tomato, and paprika. Cook, covered, for 10 minutes.
5. Add the shrimp and mussels. Cook, covered for 5 minutes or until the mussels have opened.
6. Season with salt and serve.

Lemon-Grilled Halibut with Salad

Cook time: 15 minutes	Serves: 6

Ingredients:

- 6 halibut fillets
- Juice and zest of 1 lemon
- 1 tbsp. roughly chopped fresh thyme leaves
- 1 tbsp. chopped fresh parsley
- 6 tbsps. extra-virgin olive oil, divided
- Salt and pepper to taste
- 1 fennel bulb, sliced
- ½ tsp. sea salt
- 1½ cups arugula
- ¼ cup fresh tarragon leaves
- ¼ cup chives, cut into ½-inch pieces
- ¼ cup fresh mint leaves
- ¼ cup fresh basil leaves
- Salsa verde, for garnish

Directions:

1. Season the fillets with lemon zest, thyme, and parsley. Cover and refrigerate for at least 4 hours.
2. Remove the fish from the refrigerator 15 minutes before cooking.
3. Brush the fish with 2 tbsps. olive oil and season with salt and pepper.
4. Heat 1 tbsp. oil in the Dutch oven and add the fish. Cook for 2 to 3 minutes, then flip and cook for 3 minutes or

until it is almost cooked through. Remove the pot from the heat.
5. In a bowl, add the remaining ingredients (except for the salsa verde) and season with salt and pepper to make the salad.
6. Arrange the salad on a platter. Place the fish on top.
7. Garnish the fish with salsa verde and serve.

Grilled Swordfish Steaks

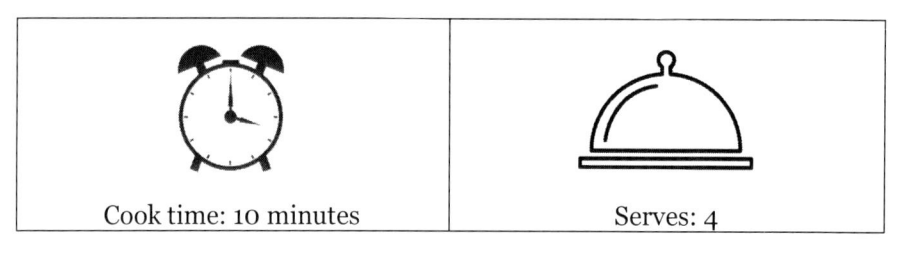

Cook time: 10 minutes	Serves: 4

Ingredients:

- 4 tbsps. extra-virgin olive oil, divided
- 2 tsps. chili powder
- 2 tsps. dried oregano, crumbled
- 1 tsp. sea salt
- ½ tsp. black pepper
- 4 swordfish steaks, cut ¾-inch thick

Directions:

1. Mix 3 tbsps. oil with chili powder, oregano, salt, and pepper. Brush the swordfish steaks with this mixture.
2. Heat the remaining 1 tbsp. olive oil in a Dutch oven. Add the fish and cook for 4 minutes. Turn and cook for a few minutes more or until both sides are browned but still moist. Serve.

Linguine with Clams

Cook time: 30 minutes	Serves: 6

Ingredients:

- 2 (16-ounce) packages linguine
- 2 tbsps. extra-virgin olive oil, divided
- 4 cloves garlic, minced
- 3 (28-ounce) cans crushed plum tomatoes
- 4 tsps. sugar
- Salt and pepper to taste
- 2 pounds littleneck clams, cleaned
- Fresh basil leaves, torn, for garnish

Directions:

1. Cook the linguine in the Dutch oven according to the directions on the package. Drain and set aside.
2. Heat 1 tbsp. oil in the Dutch oven. Add the garlic and cook for 1 minute. Stir in the tomatoes, sugar, and remaining oil. Lower heat and simmer for 20 minutes. Stir frequently. Season with salt and pepper.
3. Add the clams and cook for 5 minutes or until the clams open. Discard the unopened ones.
4. Stir in the linguine and toss to coat. Garnish and serve.

Salmon with Spinach

Cook time: 15 minutes	Serves: 6

Ingredients:

- 3 tbsps. unsalted butter
- 2 pounds fresh baby spinach
- 4 shallots, minced
- 6 salmon fillets
- 3 tbsps. fresh lemon juice
- Sea salt and pepper to taste
- 2 tsps. finely chopped fresh rosemary leaves
- 6 lemon wedges, for garnish
- Horseradish cream sauce, for garnish

Directions:

1. Preheat the oven to 325F.
2. Coat the bottom of the Dutch oven with butter. Spread the spinach leaves evenly over the butter and sprinkle with minced shallots.
3. Place the salmon fillets on the spinach, skin-side down, and drizzle with lemon juice. Season with salt, pepper, and rosemary.
4. Cover, place in the heated oven, and bake for 8 to 10 minutes.
5. Uncover the pot and check the fish. If needed, cook, uncovered for 3 to 5 minutes.
6. Garnish and serve.

Grouper with Vegetables

Cook time: 50 minutes	Serves: 4

Ingredients:

- 2 pounds grouper (fine membrane and central bone removed, cut into 1 ½-inch thick diagonal slices)
- 2 tbsps. extra-virgin olive oil
- 1 fennel bulb, thinly sliced
- 2 celery stalks, thinly sliced
- 6 shallots, skinned and chopped
- Salt and black pepper to taste
- 4 ounces butter, cut into small chunks
- 2 tsps. chopped fresh dill

Directions:

1. Heat the oil in the Dutch oven over medium heat. Add the fennel, celery, and shallots. Cook until starting to soften and transfer to a bowl.
2. Brown the fish in the oil and transfer to a plate. Return the vegetables to the pot and lay the fish on top. Season with salt and pepper.
3. Cover the Dutch oven and cook on low for 5 minutes. Transfer the vegetables to a serving plate and cover to keep warm. Cover the Dutch oven and cook the fish for 30 to 40 minutes.
4. Transfer the fish to the serving plate with vegetables.
5. Place the Dutch oven back over the heat. Return the liquid to a boil and stir in the butter.
6. Add the dill and cook until thickened. Season with salt and pepper. Pour the butter sauce over the fish. Serve.

Bouillabaisse

Cook time: 1 hour
Serves: 6

Ingredients:

- 3 tbsps. extra-virgin olive oil
- 6 garlic cloves, minced
- ¾ pound onion, diced
- 1 shallot, minced
- 1 celery stalk, minced
- 1 carrot, diced
- 1½ tbsps. tomato paste
- ½ tsp. saffron
- 1 tsp. minced basil
- 2 tbsps. minced fresh parsley
- Salt and black pepper to taste
- 1 (28-ounce) can diced tomatoes, undrained
- 2 cups clam juice
- 1 (8-ounce) jar fresh oysters, juice reserved
- 1-pound whitefish, cut into bite-size pieces
- 2½ pounds seafood mix (shrimp, clams, mussels, lobsters, scallops, crabmeat, or squid)
- 2 tbsps. chopped fresh parsley, for garnish

Directions:

1. Heat the oil in the Dutch oven. Add the garlic, onion, shallot, celery, and carrot. Sauté for 20 minutes.

2. Add the tomato paste, saffron, basil, minced parsley, salt and pepper. Mix well.
3. Add the tomatoes, clam juice, and juice from the jar of oysters. Bring to a boil, lower the heat and simmer for 15 minutes.
4. Add the oysters, whitefish, and seafood mix. Bring the pot back to a boil. Skim off any fat. Lower the heat and simmer for 15 minutes.
5. Garnish with chopped parsley and serve.

Crispy White Fish with Sauce

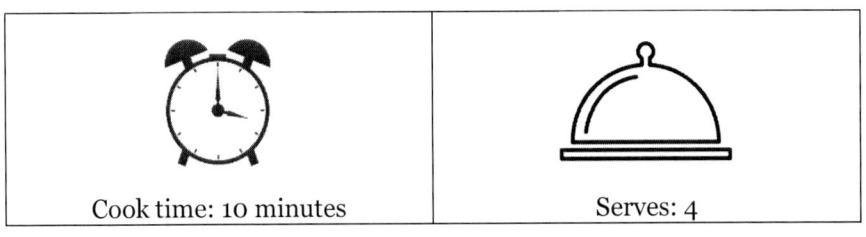

Cook time: 10 minutes	Serves: 4

Ingredients:

- ¼ cup olive oil
- ¼ cup all-purpose flour
- 4 frozen tilapia fillets, thawed
- Salt and pepper to taste
- 2 shallots, finely chopped
- 3 garlic cloves, roughly chopped
- ½ tsp. red pepper flakes
- 1 bunch fresh mint, leaves chopped
- 1 tbsp. red wine vinegar

Directions:

1. Heat the oil in the Dutch oven. Spread the flour on a plate. Season each fillet with salt and pepper and then press both sides into the flour. Shake off the excess.

2. Cook the fish 2 minutes per side. Transfer the fish to a plate.
3. Add the shallots to the pot. Add a bit of salt and cook for 2 minutes. Add the garlic and red pepper flakes and cook for 1 minute more. Turn the heat off and stir in the mint and vinegar. Deglaze the pot.
4. Spoon the sauce over the fish and serve.

Salmon Poached in Olive Oil

Cook time: 15 minutes	Serves: 4

Ingredients:

- 2 sprigs fresh sage, crushed
- 4 (1-inch) pieces lemon peel (no bitter white pith)
- 2 garlic cloves, smashed
- 4 cups olive oil (or enough to cover the fish)
- 4 (6-ounce) salmon fillets, skin on
- ¾ tsp. salt
- Grated lemon zest, for garnish
- Lemon juice, for garnish
- Flaky finishing salt, for garnish

Directions:

1. In the Dutch oven, combine the sage, lemon peel, garlic, and oil. Heat until the oil reaches 180F. Lower the heat to medium-low and keep the temperature to around 180F.
2. Season the fish with salt and then add it to the Dutch oven. If necessary, increase the heat to maintain 180F.

3. Cook for 13 to 15 minutes or until the fish is cooked. Transfer to a plate.
4. Garnish with lemon juice, zest, and salt and serve.

Halibut in Tomato Sauce with Chorizo

Cook time: 20 minutes	Serves: 4

Ingredients:

- 1½ tsps. olive oil
- 6 ounces Spanish chorizo, diced
- 1 onion, diced
- 1 garlic clove, minced
- 1 (14.5-ounce) can diced tomatoes
- 1 tsp. light brown sugar
- 2 tsp. fresh thyme leaves
- 1 tbsp. soy sauce
- 4 (6-ounce) halibut fillets
- ¼ cup chopped flat-leaf parsley, for garnish

Directions:

1. Heat the oil in the Dutch oven over medium-high heat. Add the onion, chorizo, and garlic and cook for 6 minutes or until the sausage is browned.
2. Add the tomatoes, brown sugar, thyme, and soy sauce and bring to a boil. Lower the heat to medium and simmer for 5 minutes.
3. Gently slide the fish fillets into the sauce. Cover and cook for 10 minutes or until the fish flakes easily.
4. Garnish and serve.

Roasted Cod with Potatoes and Olives

Cook time: 40 minutes | Serves: 4

Ingredients:

- 3 tbsps. olive oil
- 1 onion, halved and sliced
- 2 boiling potatoes, peeled and cut into ¼-inch-thick slices
- 1 garlic clove, minced
- ½ cup Kalamata olives cured in brine, pitted
- 4 cod fillets, about 6 ounces each
- Salt and pepper to taste
- 2 tbsps. chopped flat-leaf parsley, for garnish

Directions:

1. Preheat the oven to 450F.
2. Heat the oil in the Dutch oven. Add the onion and cook for 5 minutes.
3. Add the potatoes and garlic and cook for 10 minutes.
4. Remove from the heat and stir in olives. Put the vegetable mixture aside.
5. Season the fillets with salt and pepper and place them in the bottom of the Dutch oven. Spread the vegetable mixture over the fish. Roast, uncovered, until the fish flakes, about 20 to 25 minutes.
6. Garnish and serve.

Crispy Salmon with Lemon-Butter Sauce

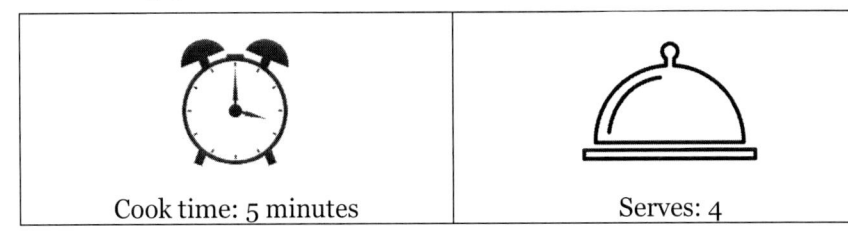

Cook time: 5 minutes	Serves: 4

Ingredients:

- 4 (4-6-oz) salmon fillets, patted dry
- Salt and pepper, to taste
- 2 tbsps. olive oil
- 1 large garlic clove, minced
- 1/3 cup dry white wine
- 2 tbsps. fresh lemon juice
- 1 lemon zested
- 3 tbsps. unsalted butter, diced
- 2 tbsps. chopped fresh dill

Directions:

1. Add 1 tbsp. oil to the Dutch oven and heat over medium heat.
2. Season the fish with salt and pepper. Add salmon flesh side down and cook for 3 to 4 minutes. Flip and cook for 3 minutes more on the skin side. Transfer to a plate.
3. Clean the Dutch oven and heat the remaining tbsp. oil.
4. Add garlic and cook for 1 minute.
5. Pour in the lemon juice and white wine. Stir for 1 minute.
6. Add lemon zest and continue to cook until slightly reduced.
7. Lower the heat and add the cubed butter, stirring after each addition.
8. Sprinkle in dill and mix.
9. Season with salt and pepper and pour the sauce over salmon fillets. Serve.

Chapter 11 Bread and Other Baked Goods

Jalapeno Corn Bread with Honey Butter

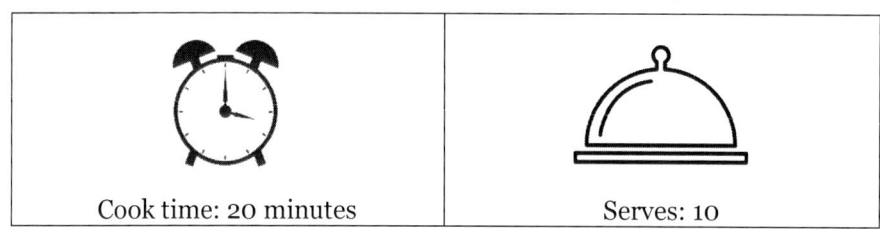

| Cook time: 20 minutes | Serves: 10 |

Ingredients:

- 1 cup cornmeal
- 1 cup all-purpose flour
- 1 tsp. baking powder
- ½ tsp. baking soda
- ½ tsp. salt
- 1 jalapeño pepper, halved and seeded, chopped and divided
- 1 scallion, thinly sliced
- 1 egg
- 1 cup buttermilk
- ¼ cup packed light brown sugar
- 8 tbsps. unsalted butter, melted, plus more for preparing the Dutch oven
- Honey, for serving

Directions:

1. Preheat the oven to 425F.
2. In a bowl, whisk the flour, cornmeal, baking powder, baking soda, and salt. Set aside.

3. Add half of the jalapeno and scallion to the dry ingredients.
4. In another bowl, whisk the egg, buttermilk, brown sugar, and melted butter. Pour the wet ingredients into the dry ingredients and lightly stir to just blend.
5. Coat a Dutch oven with melted butter. Pour the batter into the Dutch oven. Tilt the pot, so the batter lays flat. Arrange the remaining jalapeno on top.
6. Bake for 20 minutes or until golden brown. Cut the bread into slices with a spatula and serve warm with honey.

Cherry and Dark Chocolate Scones

Cook time: 25 minutes	Serves: 10

Ingredients:

- Butter for preparing the Dutch oven
- 2 cups all-purpose flour
- 4 tsps. baking powder
- ½ tsp. fine sea salt
- ¼ cup sugar, plus additional for sprinkling
- ½ cup unsalted butter, very cold and cut into small pieces
- 2 large eggs, lightly beaten
- ¾ cup whole milk, plus 2 tbsps.
- 2 tbsps. heavy cream
- ½ cup coarsely chopped dried cherries
- ½ cup semisweet chocolate chips

Directions:

1. Preheat the oven to 400F and coat the inside of the Dutch oven with butter.
2. Whisk together the flour, baking powder, salt, and sugar in a bowl. Mix the cold butter into the flour mixture until the mixture resembles fine breadcrumbs.
3. In another bowl, combine the eggs, ¾ cup milk, and cream. Stir in the dried cherries and chocolate chips. Add the egg mixture to the flour mixture and mix until a dough form.
4. Separate the dough into 10 balls of equal size. Nestle the balls of dough in the prepared Dutch oven and brush the tops with the remaining 2 tbsp. of milk.
5. Sprinkle with a bit of sugar and bake, uncovered, for 20 to 25 minutes, or until golden brown. Cover the Dutch oven if the tops brown too quickly.
6. Serve.

Honey-Jalapeno Cornbread

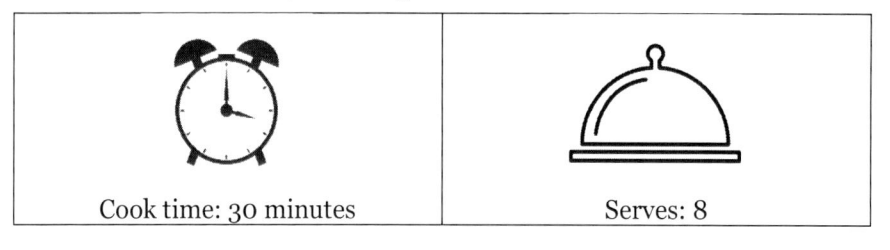

Cook time: 30 minutes	Serves: 8

Ingredients:

- ¾ cup unsalted butter, divided
- 1½ cups cornmeal
- 1½ cups all-purpose flour
- 1½ tbsp. baking powder
- 1½ tsps. salt
- 1½ cups whole milk
- ¾ cup honey
- 2 large eggs
- 1 to 2 jalapeño chiles, seeded and finely chopped

Directions:

1. Preheat the oven to 400F.
2. Melt ½ cup butter in the microwave.
3. In a bowl, whisk together the flour, cornmeal, baking powder, and salt.
4. In another bowl, whisk together the milk, honey, and eggs. Add the egg mixture to the dry mixtures and stir until just combined.
5. Stir in the jalapeno and the melted butter.
6. Melt the remaining ¼ cup of the butter in the Dutch oven. Swirl to coat. Pour the batter into the Dutch oven and transfer to the oven.
7. Bake for 25 to 30 minutes or until the edges are browned.
8. Cool, cut into wedges, and serve.

Fluffy Buttermilk Biscuits

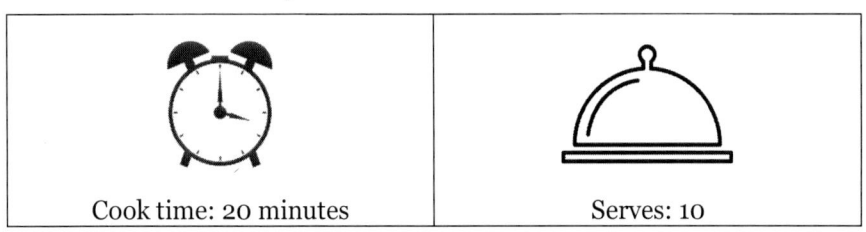

Cook time: 20 minutes	Serves: 10

Ingredients:

- 3 cups all-purpose flour
- 1 tbsp. baking powder
- 3 tbsps. sugar
- ½ tsp. fine sea salt
- ½ tsp. baking soda
- ½ cup frozen unsalted butter
- 1 cup buttermilk
- 2 tbsps. heavy cream

Directions:

1. Preheat the oven to 425F.
2. In a bowl, whisk together the flour, baking powder, sugar, salt, and baking soda. Grate the frozen butter into the dry ingredients. Toss to coat and then stir in the buttermilk to form the dough.
3. Turn the dough out onto a lightly floured cutting board and knead for 30 seconds.
4. Form the dough into a disc and then roll it out (with a rolling pin) into an even thickness. Cut the dough into rounds with a biscuit cutter.
5. Place the circles in the Dutch oven in a single layer and brush the cream over the tops.
6. Bake, uncovered, for 15 to 20 minutes or until the biscuits are golden brown.

Irish Soda Bread

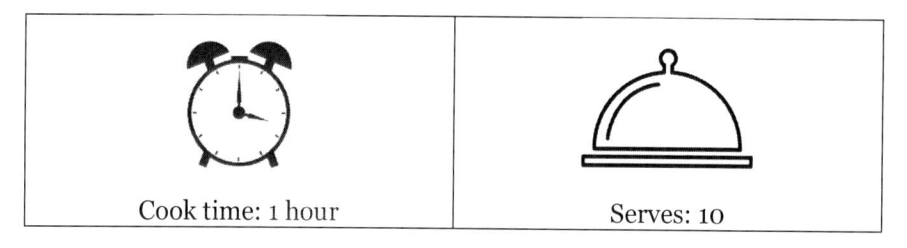

Cook time: 1 hour

Serves: 10

Ingredients:

- 4 cups wholewheat flour
- 1 cup white flour
- ½ cup rolled oats
- 1 tsp. baking soda
- 2 tsps. salt
- 2½ cups sour milk
- Cooking spray

Directions:

1. Preheat the oven to 375F.

2. In a bowl, mix the wholewheat flour, white flour, oats, baking soda, and salt. Add the sour milk and mix to form a dough.
3. Place the dough on a floured surface and knead until smooth, about 5 minutes. Use floured hands to form the dough into a round. Score a large, ½-inch deep cross into the top with a knife.
4. Lightly coat the Dutch oven with cooking spray and place the dough in the center.
5. Cover, place in the heated oven, and bake for 1 hour. Serve.

Savory Cornbread

Cook time: 20 to 25 minutes	Serves: 10

Ingredients:

- 1¼ cups yellow cornmeal
- 1¼ cups all-purpose flour
- 2 tbsps. sugar
- 1¼ tsps. baking powder
- ½ tsp. baking soda
- 1¼ tsps. salt
- 1 egg
- 1¾ cups buttermilk
- 1 cup grated Cheddar cheese
- ½ cup chopped scallions
- 3 tbsps. unsalted butter

Directions:

1. Preheat the oven to 400F.
2. In a bowl, combine the cornmeal, flour, sugar, baking powder, baking soda, and salt.
3. In another bowl, whisk together the egg and the buttermilk. Stir the egg mixture into the flour mixture.
4. Add the cheese and scallions to the flour and egg mixture and mix.
5. Melt the butter in the Dutch oven and swirl to coat the bottom and sides. Pour in the batter.
6. Cover, place in the oven, and bake for 20 to 25 minutes.

Parmesan Olive Bread

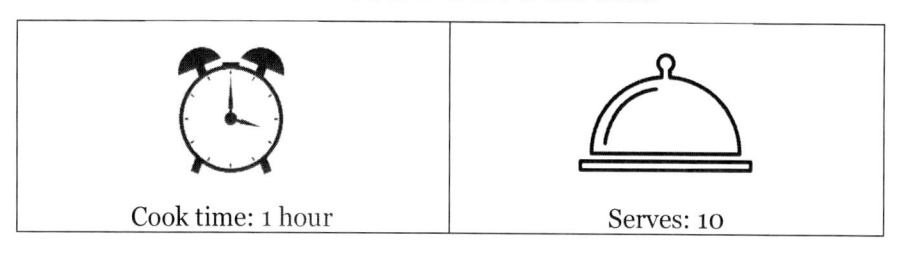

Cook time: 1 hour	Serves: 10

Ingredients:

- 4 cups all-purpose flour
- 1 tsp. instant yeast
- 1 tsp. salt
- 1½ cups water, divided
- 1¼ cups grated Parmesan cheese, divided
- ¾ cup Kalamata olives, pitted and halved
- Butter or cooking spray
- 1 tsp. extra-virgin olive oil

Directions:

1. Pour the flour, yeast, salt, and 1 cup of water into a bowl. Mix and add the remaining ½ cup water, 1 cup grated cheese, and the olives. Mix to form a dough.

2. Cover the dough with a plastic wrap and allow to rise for 2 to 4 hours or until it has doubled in size.
3. Preheat the oven to 450F. Transfer the dough to a floured surface and knead gently. Form it into a round.
4. Grease the Dutch oven with butter and place the dough in the center. Brush the top with olive oil and sprinkle with the remaining ¼ cup cheese.
5. Cover, place in the heated oven, and bake for 30 minutes.
6. Reduce the heat to 375F and bake for 30 minutes more.

Seeded Dinner Rolls

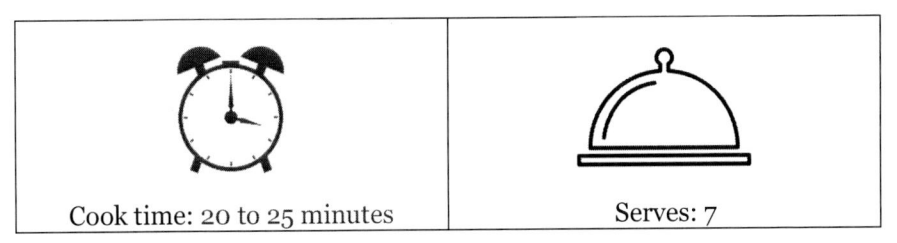

Cook time: 20 to 25 minutes	Serves: 7

Ingredients:

- ½ cup whole milk
- 3 tbsps. honey
- ¼ tsp. sea salt
- 1½ tsps. instant yeast
- 3 tbsps. cubed butter
- 1¾ cups all-purpose flour
- Butter or cooking spray, for greasing
- 1 egg white, lightly beaten
- 1 tsp. sesame seeds
- 1 tsp. poppy seeds
- 1 tsp. flaxseed

Directions:

1. In a bowl, combine the milk, honey, salt, and yeast. Add the butter and flour. Mix well. Place on a floured surface and knead for 5 minutes.
2. Transfer to a bowl and cover with plastic wrap. Allow to rise for 2 to 3 hours.
3. Preheat the oven to 400F. Grease the Dutch oven with butter.
4. Divide the dough into 7 equal pieces and make balls.
5. Place 1 ball in the center of the Dutch oven and space the other 6 balls evenly around it.
6. Brush the tops of the rolls with egg white and sprinkle with sesame seeds, poppy seeds, and flaxseed. Cover and let stand for 30 minutes.
7. Place in the preheated oven and bake for 20 to 25 minutes.

Lemon Bread

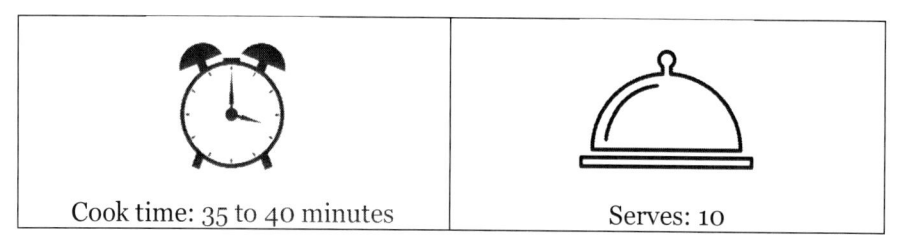

Cook time: 35 to 40 minutes | Serves: 10

Ingredients:

- 2 cups all-purpose flour
- ¼ cup poppy seeds
- 1 tbsp. baking powder
- ½ tsp. salt
- 3 eggs, lightly beaten
- 1 cup of sugar
- ½ cup of vegetable oil
- ½ cup sour cream
- ¼ cup milk

- 1 tsp. finely shredded lemon peel
- ¼ cup lemon juice
- Butter, for greasing

Directions:

1. Preheat the oven to 400F.
2. In a bowl, combine the flour, poppy seeds, baking powder, and salt. Mix well.
3. In another bowl, combine the eggs, sugar, oil, sour cream, milk, lemon peel, and lemon juice. Whisk well.
4. Add the egg mixture to the flour mixture and stir just until moistened.
5. Grease the Dutch oven with butter and spoon the batter into the pot.
6. Cover, and place in the oven. Bake for 35 to 40 minutes.

Coconut Bread

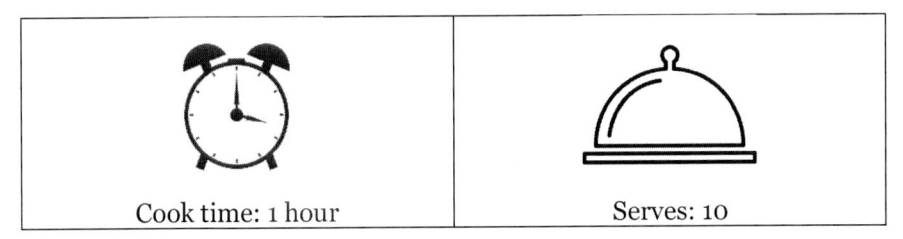

Cook time: 1 hour

Serves: 10

Ingredients:

- 3 cups all-purpose flour
- 2 tsps. baking powder
- ½ tsp. salt
- ¾ cup flaked coconut
- ½ cup unsweetened coconut milk
- 1 cup cream of coconut
- ½ cup of vegetable oil
- 3 egg whites

- ½ cup of sugar
- 1 tbsp. finely chopped lime peel
- ¼ cup lime juice
- Butter, for greasing

Directions:

1. Preheat the oven to 400F.
2. Combine the flour, baking powder, salt, and flaked coconut in a bowl.
3. In another bowl, combine the coconut milk, cream of coconut, oil, egg whites, sugar, lemon peel, and lemon juice. Add the coconut milk mixture to the flour mixture and stir just until moistened.
4. Grease the Dutch oven with butter and spoon the batter into the pot.
5. Cover, place in the oven, and bake for 1 hour.

Chapter 12 Desserts

Rhubarb & Strawberry Crisps

Cook time: 35 to 40 minutes	Serves: 6

Ingredients:

- 6 tbsps. butter, plus extra for greasing
- 3 cups sliced rhubarb
- 3 cups sliced strawberries
- ¾ cup of sugar
- 1 tbsp. cornstarch
- ¾ cup flour
- ¾ cup brown sugar
- ½ cup rolled oats
- ½ tsp. cinnamon

Directions:

1. Preheat the oven to 350F.
2. Grease a Dutch oven with butter.
3. In a bowl, combine the rhubarb, strawberries, sugar, and cornstarch. Place the fruit mixture in the Dutch oven.
4. Combine the flour, the brown sugar, and the remaining 6 tbsps. of butter and use a fork to blend until the mixture resembles coarse crumbs. Add the oats and cinnamon. Mix again. Spoon the topping over the fruit mixture.
5. Cover the pot and bake for 35 to 40 minutes. Serve.

Chocolate Bread Pudding

Cook time: 1 to 1 ¼ hours	Serves: 6

Ingredients:

- Butter, for greasing
- 8 cups sweet bread, cut into 1-inch cubes
- ¼ cup melted unsalted butter
- 1 cup of sugar
- ½ cup of cocoa powder
- 2 tsps. cinnamon
- 1 tsp. vanilla extract
- ½ tsp. almond extract
- ¼ tsp. salt
- 3 cups whole milk
- 4 large eggs
- ½ cup chocolate chips, divided

Directions:

1. Preheat the oven to 350F.
2. Grease a Dutch oven with butter.
3. Toss the bread cubes in the melted butter and arrange it in the Dutch oven. Bake for 8 to 10 minutes.
4. In a bowl, combine the sugar, cocoa powder, cinnamon, vanilla, almond extract, and salt. Add the milk and eggs and whisk to mix. Add the bread cubes and fold until moistened. Let sit for 15 to 20 minutes, folding once or twice.

5. Return half of the bread mixture to the Dutch oven. Sprinkle with ¼ cup of chocolate chips. Pour in the rest of the bread mixture and top with the remaining ¼ cup chocolate chips.
6. Cover, and return the pot to the oven. Bake for 1 to 1 ¼ hours, or until a knife inserted in the middle comes out mostly clean.

Almond Cake

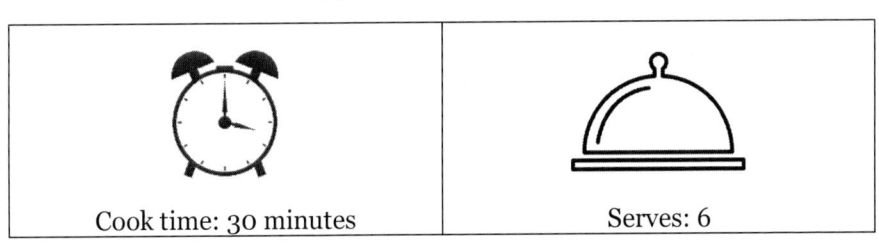

Cook time: 30 minutes	Serves: 6

Ingredients:

- 8 tbsps. unsalted butter, at room temperature, plus extra for greasing
- 7 ounces almond paste
- 3 large eggs
- 1 tbsp. rum or amaretto
- 2 drops almond extract
- ⅓ cup all-purpose flour
- ½ tsp. baking powder

Directions:

1. Preheat the oven to 350F. Grease a Dutch oven with butter.
2. In a bowl, combine the almond paste, the remaining 8 tbsp. butter, the eggs, rum, and almond extract. Mix.
3. Fold the flour and baking powder into the cake batter. Spoon into the Dutch oven.

4. Cover place the pot in the preheated oven, and bake for 30 minutes, or until a knife inserted in the middle comes out almost clean.

Mixed Berry Bake

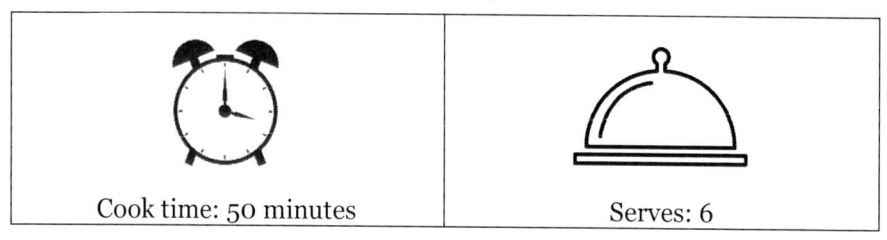

Cook time: 50 minutes	Serves: 6

Ingredients:

- Butter, for greasing
- 3 eggs
- 1 cup milk
- ¼ cup heavy cream
- ½ cup flour
- 1 tsp. vanilla extract
- ½ cup of sugar
- 2 cups mixed berries

Directions:

1. Preheat the oven to 350F and grease a Dutch oven with butter.
2. In a stand mixer, combine the eggs, milk, cream, flour, vanilla, and sugar. Blend on high for 30 seconds.
3. Pour 1 cup of batter into the Dutch oven. Cover, place in the preheated oven, and bake for 5 to 7 minutes.
4. Remove from the oven and arrange the berries on top. Pour the remaining batter over the fruit.
5. Return to the oven and bake for 45 minutes, or until golden.

Pear & Cranberry Crumble

Cook time: 45 minutes

Serves: 6

Ingredients:

- 5 large pears, peeled, cored, and sliced
- 1 pound fresh or frozen cranberries
- 2 tbsps. maple syrup
- ⅓ cup of sugar
- ½ tsp. cinnamon, divided
- ¼ tsp. nutmeg
- 1 cup rolled oats
- ⅔ cup brown sugar
- 1 stick plus 2 tbsps. butter, cut into ½-inch pieces
- ½ cup all-purpose flour
- ½ cup chopped walnuts

Directions:

1. Preheat the oven to 350F.
2. Combine the pears and cranberries in a Dutch oven. Drizzle with maple syrup. Add the sugar, ¼ tsp. cinnamon, and nutmeg. Mix well.
3. In a bowl, combine the oats, brown sugar, butter, flour, the remaining ¼ tsp. cinnamon and chopped walnuts. Mix and sprinkle the oat mixture over the fruit and pat down lightly.
4. Cover, and place the pot in the preheated oven. Bake for 45 minutes or until the pears are tender.

Classic Bread Pudding

Cook time: 1 hour	Serves: 6

Ingredients:

- Butter, for greasing
- 10 cups bread, diced into 1-inch cubes
- 3 eggs, lightly beaten
- 4 cups of milk
- ½ cup of sugar
- 1 tsp. vanilla extract
- ¼ tsp. salt

Directions:

1. Heat the oven to 325F. Grease a Dutch oven with butter and add the bread cubes.
2. In a bowl, combine the eggs, milk, sugar, vanilla, and salt. Pour the egg mixture over the bread cubes. Press down slightly with a spoon to lightly moisten the bread. Let sit for 15 to 20 minutes, folding the mixture once or twice.
3. Cover the pot and place it in the heated oven. Cook for 1 hour or until golden brown.

Deconstructed Apple Pie

Cook time: 25 minutes

Serves: 6

Ingredients:

- 2 tbsps. butter
- 5 cups apple slices
- 1 tsp. ground cinnamon
- ½ tsp. ground nutmeg
- ½ tsp. ground cardamom
- ⅓ cup pure maple syrup
- ½ cup all-purpose flour
- ½ tsp. baking powder
- ⅛ tsp. salt
- Whipped cream, for serving

Directions:

1. Melt the butter in the Dutch oven. Add the apples and cook for 2 minutes. Coat well with the butter.
2. Add the cinnamon, nutmeg, and cardamom and mix well. Cover and cook for 4 minutes or until aromatic.
3. Stir in the maple syrup and lower the heat to medium-low. Cover and cook for 10 minutes.
4. In a bowl, whisk the flour, baking powder, and salt to combine. Set aside.
5. Stir the apples once more and spread them into an even layer.
6. Sprinkle the flour mixture evenly over the apples. Turn the heat to medium and cover the pot. Cook for 5 minutes. Stir the mixture to combine.
7. Serve, topped with whipped cream.

Mango Sticky Rice

Cook time: 40 minutes | Serves: 6

Ingredients:

- 1 ½ cups of sushi rice
- 1 (14-ounce) can full-fat coconut milk
- 1/3 cup sugar
- ¼ tsp. salt
- 2 mangos, sliced
- 1 tbsp. toasted sesame seeds

Directions:

1. Pour the rice into a fine-mesh sieve and set it over a bowl. Fill the bowl with water and slosh the rice with your hand for a few minutes. Let sit for 3 hours, then drain.
2. Set the sieve with the rice over a Dutch oven of simmering water. Cover the pot and steam the rice for 30 to 40 minutes or until tender. Transfer the cooked rice to a bowl and cover with a plate.
3. While the rice cools, in a saucepan, combine the coconut milk, sugar, and salt. Cook, occasionally stirring for 1 minute. Turn off the heat.
4. To serve, scoop, and press the rice into a measuring cup to mold. Turn it onto a serving plate and drizzle the coconut milk sauce over the rice. Fan the mango slices on top and sprinkle with toasted sesame seeds. Serve.

Cookies and Cream Ice Cream Cake

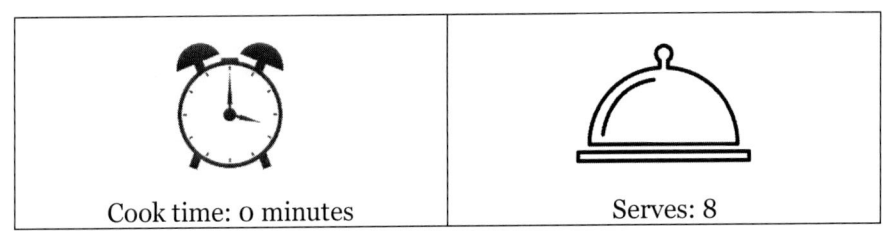

Cook time: 0 minutes

Serves: 8

Ingredients:

- 1-gallon cookies and cream ice cream
- 1 (19-ounce) package chocolate sandwich cookies
- 4 tbsps. unsalted butter, melted
- 1 (16-ounce) jar fudge topping
- 1 (8-ounce) container frozen whipped topping, thawed

Directions:

1. Set the ice cream on the counter for 30 minutes to soften.
2. Chop the sandwich cookies well (about 36 cookies). Reserve 1 cup of the chopped cookies for topping the cake. Put the remaining cookies in a Dutch oven with the melted butter. Stir to combine. Then press down to form a crust.
3. Spread the softened ice cream over the cookie crust. Cover the pot and freeze for 2 hours. Pour the fudge sauce over the ice cream layer and freeze for 1 hour more. Spread the whipped topping over the fudge layer and top with the reserved chopped cookies. Freeze overnight or at least 8 hours.
4. Remove the Dutch oven from the freezer 20 minutes before serving. Serve.

Buttermilk Cherry Clafoutis

Cook time: 35 minutes

Serves: 6

Ingredients:

- Unsalted butter, for preparing the Dutch oven
- 1-pound sweet black cherries
- 4 eggs
- ½ cup granulated sugar
- ¼ cup packed light brown sugar
- 1 cup buttermilk
- 2 tsps. vanilla extract
- ¼ tsp. salt
- ¾ cup all-purpose flour
- Powdered sugar, for dusting
- Vanilla ice cream, for serving (optional)

Directions:

1. Preheat the oven to 375F and coat the Dutch oven with butter.
2. Stem and pit the cherries and place in the Dutch oven.
3. In a bowl, whisk the eggs, granulated sugar, brown sugar, buttermilk, vanilla, salt, and flour until smooth. Pour the filling over the cherries.
4. Bake for 10 minutes. Lower the temperature to 350F and bake for 25 minutes more. Dust with powdered sugar and serve with ice cream.

Chapter 13 Staples and Sauces

Mild Red Enchilada Sauce

Cook time: 10 minutes	Makes: 3 ½ cups

Ingredients:

- 2 tbsps. lard, such as bacon grease
- ¼ cup mild chili powder
- 1 tbsp. ground cumin
- 1 tsp. garlic powder
- ½ tsp. dried oregano
- 1 (15-ounce) can tomato sauce
- 1½ cups of beef stock
- 2 tsps. cornstarch
- 1 tsp. salt

Directions:

1. Melt the lard in the Dutch oven. Add the chili powder, cumin, garlic powder, and oregano. Cook for 1 minute and then add the tomato sauce.
2. In a cup, whisk the beef stock and cornstarch to make a slurry. Immediately add the slurry to the tomato mixture. Increase the heat and cook for 5 minutes. Stirring well. Add the salt and use.

Smoky Paprika Cream Sauce

Cook time: 5 minutes

Makes: ¾ cup

Ingredients:

- 3 tbsps. unsalted butter
- ½ tsp. grated lemon zest
- 2½ tsps. smoked paprika
- ½ tsp. salt
- ¼ cup chicken stock
- 2 tbsps. lemon juice
- ⅓ cup heavy cream, plus more as needed

Directions:

1. Melt the butter in the Dutch oven. Then add the lemon zest, paprika, and salt. Cook for 1 minute, then add the chicken stock and bring to a simmer.
2. Turn off the heat and add the lemon juice and heavy cream. Simmer for a few minutes for a thinner sauce and add more cream. Serve.

Caramel Sauce

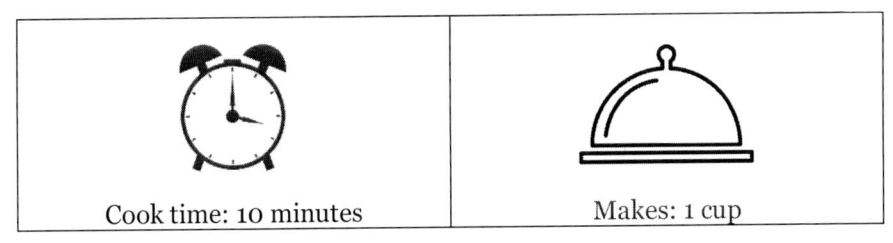

Cook time: 10 minutes	Makes: 1 cup

Ingredients:

- 1 cup of sugar
- 3 tbsps. water
- ½ cup heavy cream
- 4 tbsps. unsalted butter
- ½ tsp. salt

Directions:

1. Combine the sugar and water in a Dutch oven. Bring the mixture to a simmer without stirring. Once the sugar dissolves, cook for 3 minutes more or until the mixture gets an amber color. Remove from the heat and add the heavy cream. Mix for 1 minute.
2. Add the butter and whisk until you get a smooth sauce. Stir in the salt and use.

Chile Nacho Cheese Sauce

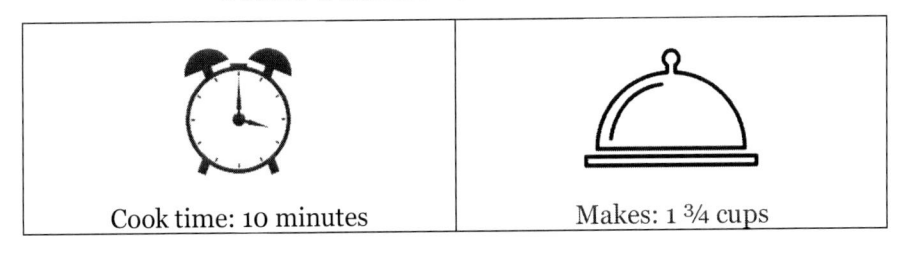

Cook time: 10 minutes	Makes: 1 ¾ cups

Ingredients:

- 2 tbsps. unsalted butter
- 2 tbsps. all-purpose flour
- 1½ cups whole milk
- 1 cup shredded cheddar cheese
- ¾ tsp. salt
- 1 (4-ounce) can diced Hatch chiles

Directions:

1. Melt the butter in the Dutch oven. Add the flour and cook for 1 minute. Add the milk and cook for 1 minute more.
2. Turn off the heat and add the cheese and salt. Mix until smooth. Stir in the chilies and serve.

Peanut Satay Sauce

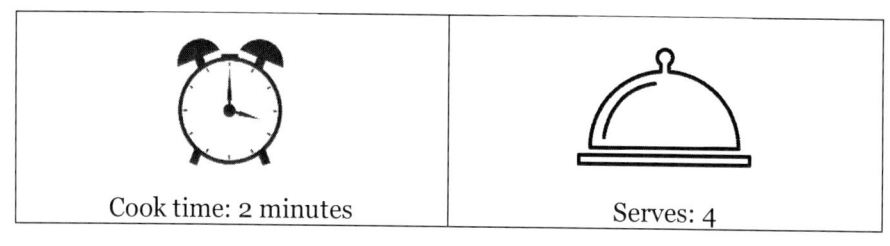

Cook time: 2 minutes	Serves: 4

Ingredients:

- 1 cup unsweetened coconut milk
- ½ cup creamy peanut butter
- 2 tbsps. low-sodium soy sauce
- 2 tbsps. packed light brown sugar
- ½ tsp. ground ginger
- ½ tsp. dried garlic
- 1½ tbsps. lemon juice
- ½ tsp. salt

Directions:

1. In the Dutch oven, whisk the coconut milk, peanut butter, soy sauce, brown sugar, ginger, and garlic until smooth, about 2 minutes. Bring the mixture to a boil and lower the heat. Continue to whisk until the mixture starts to thicken.
2. Turn off the heat and whisk the lemon juice and salt. Serve.

Enchilada Sauce

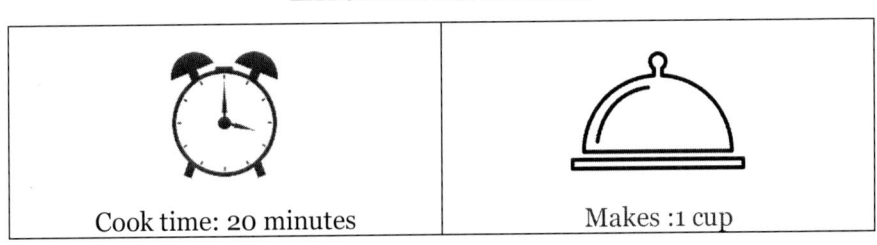

Cook time: 20 minutes | Makes :1 cup

Ingredients:

- 2 tbsps. olive oil
- 1 tbsp. minced garlic
- 2 tbsps. all-purpose flour
- 1 tsp. dried oregano
- 1 tsp. ground cumin
- 1 tsp. chili powder
- 2 cups vegetable broth
- 1 tbsp. tomato paste
- 1 tbsp. distilled white vinegar
- ½ tsp. salt

Directions:

1. Heat the olive oil in the Dutch oven. Add the garlic and cook for 30 seconds. Whisk in the flour and sauté for 2 minutes.
2. Add the oregano and cumin. Sauté for 2 minutes and add the chili powder and sauté for 1 minute more.

3. Stir in the broth, tomato paste, vinegar, and salt. Cover the pot and cook for 5 minutes.
4. Lower the heat and stir. Cover and cook for 10 minutes. Cool and serve.

Lemon Garlic Butter Sauce

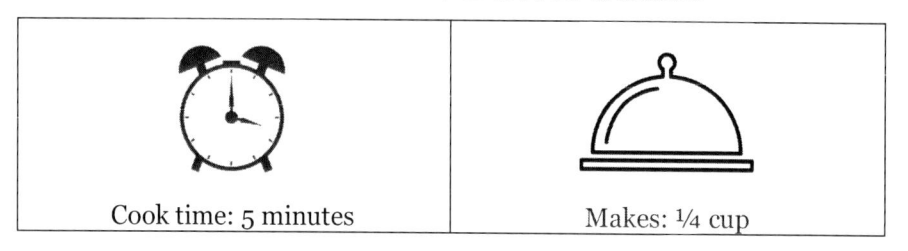

Cook time: 5 minutes	Makes: ¼ cup

Ingredients:

- ¼ cup butter
- 2 garlic cloves, crushed
- 1 tbsp. lemon juice
- 2 tsps. grated lemon zest

Directions:

1. In the Dutch oven, stir together the butter, garlic, lemon juice, and lemon zest. Cook for 2 minutes.
2. Turn off the heat and cook for 1 minute more. Serve.

Béchamel Sauce

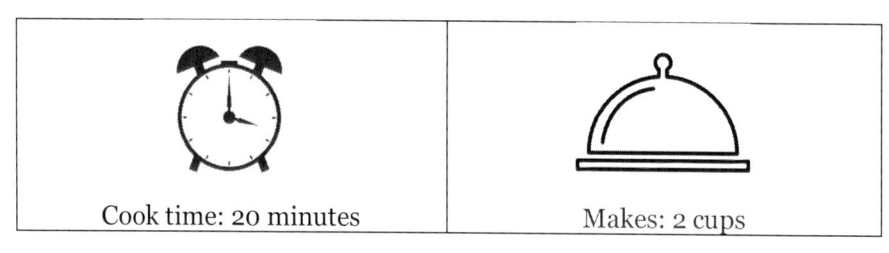

Cook time: 20 minutes	Makes: 2 cups

Ingredients:

- 2 tbsps. olive oil
- 2 tbsps. all-purpose flour
- 2 ½ cups unsweetened coconut milk
- 1 tsp. salt
- 1 tbsp. black pepper

Directions:

1. Heat the Dutch oven. Add the oil and flour and cook for 3 minutes more. Do not let the flour brown.
2. Stir in the coconut milk, salt, and pepper. Raise the heat to be medium and cover the pot. Cook for 10 minutes more. Stir and cook for 5 minutes more. Serve.

Arrabbiata Sauce

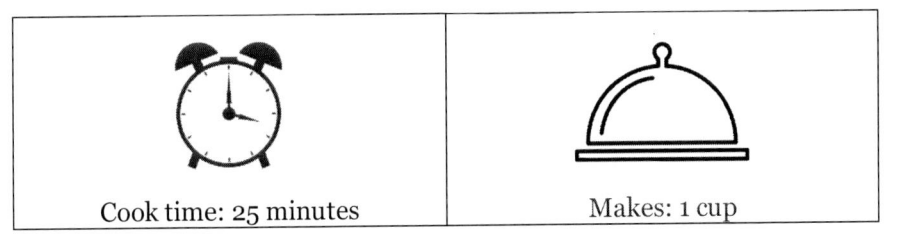

Cook time: 25 minutes	Makes: 1 cup

Ingredients:

- 2 tbsps. olive oil
- 1 tbsp. minced garlic
- 3 cups finely chopped tomato
- 1 tbsp. tomato paste
- 2 tsps. red pepper flakes
- 1 tsp. salt
- 1 tsp. black pepper
- 2 tbsps. chopped fresh basil

Directions:

1. Heat the oil in the Dutch oven. Add the garlic and cook for 10 seconds.
2. Stir in the tomato, tomato paste, red pepper flakes, salt, and black pepper.
3. Turn the heat to medium and cover. Cook for 15 to 20 minutes or until the sauce reduces slightly.
4. Mix well. Add ¼ cup water and deglaze. Bring the mixture to a boil.
5. Stir in the basil and serve.

Jalapeno Mango Chutney

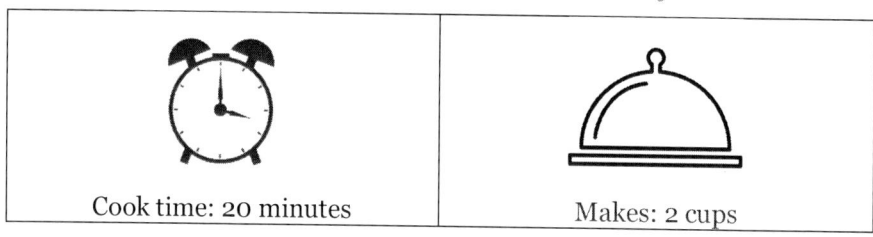

Cook time: 20 minutes	Makes: 2 cups

Ingredients:

- 1 (1-package) frozen mango chunks
- ¼ cup powdered sugar
- 2 jalapeno peppers, chopped
- ½ tsp. ground cumin
- ¼ tsp. salt

Directions:

1. In the Dutch oven, stir together the mango, sugar, jalapeno peppers, cumin, and salt. Cover and cook for 5 minutes or until the mango begins to release its juice.
2. Lower the heat and cover the pot. Cook for 10 to 12 minutes.
3. Mash the mixture with a food masher. Remove from the heat, cool, and serve.

Conclusion

Whether it is on the home fireplace hearth or outdoors, the Dutch oven produces great-tasting food with minimum effort. This cookbook includes Dutch oven recipes that include breakfast, fish, seafood, beef, pork, lamb, poultry, soup, stews, bread, and desserts. The recipes are simple yet delicious and use easy to find ingredients. Whether you are throwing a party for your family or camping with friends, a Dutch oven will make cooking simple, unique, and enjoyable.

Made in United States
North Haven, CT
28 December 2023